Any Fool Can Be a.....
Pig Farmer

by
James Robertson

The Good Life Press LTD

ANY FOOL CAN BE A.....
PIG FARMER

By

JAMES ROBERTSON

Originally Published by Farming Press 1975
Published by The Good Life Press Ltd. 2010

ISBN 978 1 90487 1 712
A catalogue record for this book is available from
the British Library.

Published by
The Good Life Press Ltd.
The Old Pigsties
Clifton Fields
Lytham Road
Preston
PR4 0XG

www.goodlifepress.co.uk
www.homefarmer.co.uk

Front cover designed by Rachel Gledhill
Printed and bound in the UK by
CPI Mackays, Chatham ME5 8TD

Preface

The sweetish Spanish plonk flowed free and the perspiring waitress placed a brick-like slice of gateau in front of me. Preparation for the annual farmers' junket had caused me half an hour's agony as I scrubbed the ingrained agricultural dirt from underneath my fingernails and resurrected my dinner jacket. At home sow number 36 was due to farrow, a worry which now distracted me from my effort to sparkle at my neighbour, the wife of a solicitor.

'Tell me,' she asked; 'have you thought about your children's education?'

She, dear lady, was trying hard too. I leant forward to enlighten her about the financial problems of pig farmers, and as I did so a pig louse fell out of my hair. Huge and squat, it landed on her side plate with a clatter, turned itself upright and grinned at her. There was a moment's frozen silence before her scream cut through the conversation and all eyes turned on me.

I fled home with my wife rather sooner than we expected.

That was one of the big troubles about pigs. Apart from trying to bankrupt me they could also create truly monumental social embarrassment.

Pigs...not such a Bad Idea

'Guts for sausage skins, skin for suede shoes and suitcases, trotters for glue; in fact the only part of the animal that we don't use is the squeak. Ha ha.'

'Ho Ho,' we all echoed dutifully. If you're in advertising and the client cracks a joke, you laugh, loud and long. It does not matter if, as in this case, the first cracker of that particular joke was Noah when he was rolling out his last barrel of salted pork. The client pays the bills.

Come to think of it, pigs were not such a bad idea. I had recently had the bad experience of being involved in a pitch for a new account. Our team had gone along to the prospective client's office (not the sausage king), clutching the result of hours of midnight oil and much genius which was going to wrest his business from one of our competitors. The client had stood up to say a few words before we started our presentation. He went on for about an hour - a droning incomprehensible load of twaddle. The creative people in our team - which means those who draw the pictures and write the words - started to play battleships, but my main function was to sit there and behave as if everything he said should have been engraved on tablets of gold.

We won the account which meant that a large portion of my working life would henceforth be spent with the most totally mind-blowing bore with whom I had ever been thrown in contact.

My boss was not prepared to transfer me from the account. Word of this client had got around and I had received a letter of thanks from the rival agent who had previously handled him. The only way of retaining sanity was to look around for another job. My wife and I were both in advertising and so I first looked around for another job within the business. No luck. I received the odd offer on condition that I would bring some business with me to the new employer. The only business that I thought I could steal was the bore which rather defeated the purpose of

4

any move. We looked around for something else.

This was in the early seventies; at the height of the period when it was fashionable in London to disappear into some rural fastness in order to find one's soul. We thought we were already halfway there, having bought a semi in the depths of the Kent countryside from where we would both commute to the West End every day. It was rural England at its duckiest. The entire population disappeared on weekdays as they were sucked into London, leaving their bijou cottages empty and deserted. At weekends the pub would be packed by people with artificial straw in their hair discussing the state of the crops and the weather over their pints of scrumpy and country wine.

The one genuine local doubled as the postman and the village Peeping Tom. He would be surrounded by a semi-circle of admirers plying him with gins and tonic - he had sufficient legitimacy to be able to drink what he liked - while they tried to brush up their rural accents. The landlord, a retired wing commander, always wore gumboots. No authentic peasant would have dreamed of crossing the threshold of such a suburban waterhole. The only contact was late on a Saturday night when the local youths would roar up in the pub car park on their motor bikes and let down the tyres of the BMWs and Volvos that filled it.

We were then invited to stay on a real farm for the weekend. It was a revelation. The true countrydweller dressed up to go to the pub. He did not dress down. And farming seemed to be such a delightfully easy way to make a living. You tugged a few teats or threw some seeds on the ground. Milk or wheat would then appear. You did not have to think too hard and you did not have to make anything. Nature did it all for you. In addition, the state would give you vast sums of money to keep you in business, no matter how little work was done or how inefficient you were.

Those were the days when the 'feather-bedded farmer' was part of the national lore.

No more stuffy offices; you could live a healthy outdoor life and there seemed to be an abundant supply of gnarled old men with totally incomprehensible accents to take charge of any actual work that had to be done in exchange for a pittance. Apart from the ordinary subsidies, there was another source of government money called a grant, which meant that the state would buy you a tractor or any other bit of equipment to allow you to drive round the fields in the sunshine and admire the hedges, or do whatever else is done in fields with a tractor.

It was true that, even in those days, some people seemed to feel the need to go to agricultural colleges of one sort or another, but farms had produced food before the invention of the BSc(Agric) and it was obvious that a quick-witted adman would have little difficulty in showing a few country clods how to run a farm in an efficient and business-like manner. It would be a doddle. A few hundred acres and a nice house would set us up for a pleasant, idle life.

There turned out to be a snag. Although there seemed to be a great deal of land lying about not doing very much, the owners wanted unreasonably large amounts of money for it. Our two thousand pounds, even in 1971, did not impress the estate agents and, although we could have borrowed the money to buy a farm, the Bank Rate stood at a prohibitive 5 per cent. After a few days, it became obvious that farming would be out unless we won the football pools and neither my wife nor I have ever understood how to do them.

We then thought about guesthouses and throwing pots. But for one you needed charm and for the other, talent. Then someone suggested market gardening. It was a possibility, being farming of a sort, but if there was one thing we disliked more than commuting, it was gardening. We managed to rear the finest crop of nettles in Kent, but the market for nettles had never been large. Farming to us meant animals, particularly cows. It meant lording it over broad acres; wandering round in a Land Rover looking scruffy but superior. You can't look superior because you grow a few lettuces for a living.

Then a client (not the boring client) started to talk about

his sausages and the raw material from which they were made. Over the crepes suzette at lunch I quizzed him about the subject. When he joined his company twenty years earlier, he had been shown round a pig farm so he knew all about the subject. Pigs apparently made a fortune. One sow would produce about thirty piglets a year. Pigs cost nothing to feed as all they ate was table scraps. You could keep fifty sows inside one old Nissen hut or something similar. Mathematics over coffee proved that one Nissen hut would yield an income of £15,000 a year. On that sort of income, we could easily afford to buy a nice country house and hire some old rustic to do the dirty work for us. Admen are not complete fools, however, and it seemed to me that there had to be a snag somewhere, otherwise everybody would be keeping pigs. The client was quite certain all the same. He had even once thought of keeping pigs himself in his garden but the Camden planning officials had been unenthusiastic.

That evening I managed to convince my wife. We would become pig farmers. They were not cows, it was true, but they were authentic farm animals and definitely a cut above a lettuce or a cucumber. I could see myself communing with a pig over a farm gate after a day's work with the sun setting behind the midden but I could never visualise achieving much of a rapport with a vegetable.

The decision made, there were several steps to be taken. First was to hand in my notice. My boss showed a distressing lack of emotion. Then have a chat with the bank manager and find a farm. Perhaps, somewhere along the line, even try to find out a little about pigs.

Looking back, the interview with the bank manager was most astonishing. I went into his office and he looked at me benignly. I felt rather more apprehensive. I did not know if West End banks did much farm financing. 'I've come to see you about arranging an overdraft.'

'Oh yes. And how much do you want?'

'I'm not really sure yet. It depends.'

7

'I see. Right. Let's start at the beginning. What do you do?'

'Well, at the moment, I work for an advertising agency....'

'And you want me to finance you into setting up your own,' he interrupted.

'No. I want you to finance me in starting up a pig farm.'

'A pig farm! You want to get away from it all, do you?'

'No. I just want to start pig farming.'

'Are you sure you don't want to grow tomatoes in Cornwall? Most of my clients come to me wanting to grow tomatoes in Cornwall and I never lend them any money. It's one of my principles.'

'No, not tomatoes, pigs.'

'Chickens?'

'No. Pigs.'

He leaned forward in his chair. 'Right, now we've established that pigs is what you're going to do, let's look at the financial aspect.' He got out a sheet of paper and we worked profit projections and cash flows based on the sausage client's figures. We arrived at the figure of £15,000 and sat back and looked at it with a certain degree of smugness. 'Yes,' he said, 'that looks like quite an interesting proposition. Do you know very much about pigs?'

'I don't know very much just at the moment; but I intend to take a correspondence course.'

'Oh good. The Danes. They're the chaps.'

'I beg your pardon?'

'You know. Sizzle, sizzle. Danish bacon, lean and tasty. Or is that Irish? Anyway, it doesn't matter much. Why don't you go to Denmark for a few weeks to learn about pigs?'

'I can't really afford it.'

'Oh. Don't worry about that. I'm sure we can find the money. After all, the best way to protect our investment is for us to make sure that you know what you are doing.'

'Security. Won't you want some security?'

'Well, I suppose you could always drop in the deeds of your farm when you buy it.'

I have since discovered that not all bank managers are like him. In fact, when he retired about three months later, we had to move our account fairly smartly and chose a bank about four hundred miles from the farm, reasoning that what the manager could not see, he would not worry about.

Once our finances were in order I sent for the course in pig farming. I had mentioned it on the spur of the moment to the bank manager but it seemed to be quite a good idea. The course consisted of a series of pamphlets with examination questions at the end of each pamphlet. These required the pupil to regurgitate large chunks of the course which were then sent away to be marked. After a rocky start, I discovered that you lost a mark if you deviated from the original text by as much as a comma during the regurgitation. I learned to copy it out precisely and my papers would return marked, 'excellent work - you clearly have the intelligence to benefit from our advanced courses in swine husbandry, home economics and Swahili which will be available to you at a five per cent discount.'

The course, looking back at it, was of no value whatsoever but, at the time, I hung on its every word as if it was the Bible. It had an annoying habit of assuming a certain amount of basic knowledge which I did not possess. My knowhow on pigs was limited to the belief that you took this little piggy to market and that this little piggy ate roast beef. I learned too (obvious information that had not occurred to me) that where there were little pigs as well as mummy pigs, there had to be daddy pigs. Blue pigs, I read, tended to be fat. I had always assumed that the whole essence of pigginess lay in being fat rather like the Empress of Blandings. I had never even heard of a blue pig.

It said other surprising things like 'hams should be full and rounded.' Outside of a sandwich, I was not very sure of the usual location of a ham. And what could they be if they weren't full and rounded. Empty and triangular? 'The back of a pig should be long.' Six inches? Six feet? Six miles? How was I supposed to know? It was all rather bemusing.

9

Pigs, apparently, ate things other than table scraps. Strange things like cassava, sorghum and decorticated groundnut meal, all of which was classified by its dry matter content and its starch and protein equivalents. When I eventually found out what all that meant, I discovered that the whole system of classifying feeds had changed so I had to start again. There was even a horror story about the danger of feeding table scraps. The course compiler had fed his pigs on swill from the local hospital until his herd was struck by an epidemic of sleeping sickness. After much investigation, it turned out that the patients were stuffing their sleeping pills and all sorts of other drugs into their mashed potatoes which were ending up inside the pigs.

Sows farrowed (instead of giving birth) in curious iron cages called crates; otherwise they sat on their young and squashed them which seemed remarkably stupid. Piglets lived in a nursery called a creep when they were with their mothers and then they turned into weaners and lived in pools. A maiden gilt was a virgin sow. There was a whole new jargon to be learned. The course also went into great detail about the types of housing that were, apparently, essential for the animals' survival, all of which were a far cry from the original Nissen hut.

However, I solidly ploughed my way through the course and sent away for the final pamphlets. I received a letter back containing a diploma stating that I had graduated as a fully qualified pig farmer with first-class honours. There was an apology for the fact that they had run out of copies of the final lectures which would be forwarded to me as soon as they had been reprinted but, meantime, they had pleasure in enclosing a lecture on rabbit rearing as a substitute. I never did discover what I had missed as the correspondence school went bankrupt before they were able to post me the remaining lectures.

What a Pigsty!

The most critical part of changing an office worker into a pig farmer was finding a farm. Using the office duplicator we sent a letter out to most of the estate agents in England asking for details of any properties on their books with a minimum of three acres of land up to a maximum price of £15,000. This was the balmy days before the property boom of the early seventies when God was in his Heaven and Harold Wilson was his representative on earth.

We then sat back and waited to take our pick from the flood. The estate agents lived down to their reputation. They sent details of properties ranging from castles in Spain to penthouse flats in Mayfair. Others, having at least skimmed our letter, sent details of thousand-acre farms in East Anglia which were open to offers. Some pretended that they had computers and were unable to understand our letter; they sent back forms to fill in, listing every requirement known to man down to whether the dog (Yes/No) preferred an inside/outside kennel. Once they received our forms back, they would send details of castles in Spain just like everybody else.

We decided to go about farm hunting in a systematic manner and split the country into areas. Each Saturday we would set off at 6 am towards our designated area armed with half a dozen likely looking sets of property details. The foul tempers induced by having to force ourselves out of bed at such an ungodly hour would not be helped by the maniacal chucklings of the disc jockey on the car radio as he urged listeners to rise from sleep and greet the beautiful morning at half-past eleven.

We would get to the central point of the area, stop for a cup of coffee and then my wife would bring out the map and mark the farms on it. We would return to the car and from then on the conversation would have a certain predictability.

'Will you slow down! How do you expect me to read the map at this speed?'

'I'm not driving fast. Which way at this crossroad?'

'Where are we?'

'That's what I'm asking you, dear. You've got the map.'

'Have we been through Beaworthy/Marston Magna/Chippenham/Diss yet?'

'I don't know.'

'Well what was that place we've just been through?'

'I don't know. You're the one with the map.'

'But I can't read the bloody thing with you driving like a lunatic.'

'You mean you can't read a simple map.'

'Oh shut up. See if you can read the damn thing.'

'We're probably half way to John O'Groats by now.'

'That's it. Left down there.'

'That's not a road. You've lost us.'

'I know it's not a road. That's the farm we've come to look at.'

'Oh, I see. But I can't get the car down a donkey track like that.'

'You mean down the imposing, gently undulating entrance drive.'

'We'll have to walk down there.'

'I'm not walking. I'll get my shoes muddy.'

'Put on your boots.'

'I haven't got my boots.'

'I don't believe it. Farm hunting and she hasn't brought her boots.'

'You said that you hadn't taken them out of the car.'

A brief spat would develop and we'd grind our way down the lane between high hedges and jam on the brakes when we reached the bottom.

'Where's the house?'

'There.'

'No, the farmhouse, not that cattleshed.'

'I've a horrible feeling that the cattleshed is the farmhouse.'

'Don't be silly. Good Lord, you're right. There are curtains on the windows. Quick. Turn the car and let's get out of here. This is a waste of time.'

When we couldn't get the car turned round fast enough and the proprietor entrapped us into listening to his sales pitch, we sometimes managed to pick up a thing or two about pigs. If, of course, we were able to understand the accent. Many of these places were run-down farms whose owners had just grown too old to work them properly. Many of the vendors and their accents were born in Queen Victoria's rural England. Most of them had a fat sow or two in a sty behind the house and we would lean over and gravely examine these hulking hand-tame beasts while the owner scratched his ear.

We were once a witness to an astonishing example of porcine genius. This particular owner was selling because he had been attacked by that ubiquitous agricultural affliction, farmer's back. He kept his three sows in an orchard and we watched them work in unison to get an overburdened apple tree rocking so that it shed its fruit into their waiting jaws.

We discovered that pig farmers fell into three kinds. Those who bred pigs, those who fattened them and those who combined both operations. We decided to become breeders for the simple reason that it was cheaper. The fattener needed a considerable amount of capital to buy all those piglets produced by the breeder and then needed to tie up more money in feeding costs before he got a return on selling the finished pigs. The breeder had an easier time of it because his output spent most of its time receiving free sustenance from mother's teats and less time on expensive meal.

Far from living on table scraps, it was becoming apparent that a pig needed a carefully balanced diet to grow fat and produce its offspring efficiently. No doubt it had something to do with those mysterious 'dry matters' and 'protein equivalents.' I had visions of having to work out complicated equations and then juggle around with test tubes over boiling cauldrons to make sure that the feed was properly balanced and prepared. Fortunately, there turned out to be benevolent institutions called compounders who were willing to do it all for you - at a price.

We drifted through the rural slums of the West Country and East Anglia. Nothing that suited us seemed to be within our price range. Part of the trouble was that my wife and I had different ideas about what we were looking for. She wanted a vaguely waterproof house and I wanted a reasonable set of buildings that could be easily converted to house pigs. We found lots of cottages with honeysuckle over the door about which she would rave while I looked gloomily at the garden shed. Alternatively there were lovely sets of buildings with ruinous houses about which I would be quite happy. I was never too secure about the forty-odd acres of bottomless bog which lapped evilly behind all those with good barns.

Then one morning we hit the Welsh borders and found two places that would suit us. We spent the weekend trotting between the two and dithering in a local pub. One was a small cottage with a reasonable set of buildings set on the banks of a river. The other was an enormous farmhouse which had lorded it over a couple of hundred acres. The farm was being sold off separately and the house, which was split into two, was being sold with four acres and a seemingly endless collection of barns, pens, byres, sties and cowsheds which illustrated the various developments in farm architecture over the past three hundred years. The owner was selling cheaply because he intended to emigrate the following month and because most prospective buyers were discouraged by the sheer quantity of the buildings.

At dinner in the pub that night we tried to come to a decision.

'What do you think?' asked my wife over the turnip soup.

'One thing we must do is try to be logical about which we choose.' The turnip soup was just as bad as it sounds.

'That'll be the day.'

'The one on the river is prettier and it's got rather more

14

land.'

'The house is a lot smaller.' The soup was replaced by a hunk of lamb which proved that even the fabled Welsh lambs sometimes died of old age before they could reach the slaughterhouse.

'We'll need a larger house soon.' This was the first time that we were to discover that all great changes in our way of life only took place when my wife was pregnant.

'The farmhouse will give us a lot more for our money.'

'But the roof leaks. It housed evacuees during the war and all the bedrooms are split into tiny cubicles.'

'And it is set in beautiful countryside with redundant slag heaps stretching as far as the eye can see.'

'With a fine view of the crematorium.' We bounced our teeth off the lamb for a few moments in silence. I thought of an objection to the cottage.

'I will bash my head on every ceiling. I mean the ceilings in the cottage are so low that some of them have already got bloodstains on them and the man selling it is only about five foot four.'

'Perhaps he's got tall friends.'

'The farmhouse is split into two which means that we can let half of it off.'

'It's been on the market for months which means that it'll be a sod to sell when we decide to get rid of it.'

The conversation meandered on down to the local Chinese takeaway where we went for an after-dinner snack. As we munched our way through double portions of sweet-and-sour pork to try to kill the fishy taste of of the pub lemon soufflé we came to a decision. We would send a surveyor into the farmhouse.

Survey reports always read like horror stories, but this one turned out to be really special. He found dry rot, wet rot and death-watch beetle. He took one look at all the slag heaps and found subsidence as well. After several pages of this catalogue of horrors, he stated that the house was in reasonable condition considering the use to which it was to be put. This peculiar remark led me to telephone the surveyor to find out what he meant. He thought we were going to house pigs in it.

The survey was so bad that it proved invaluable. The vendor was desperate to get the place off his hands before he set off for New Zealand and he knocked about a third off his asking price. We did not tell the man that, by now, we were almost as desperate to buy as he was to sell. During the search of the West Country we had sold our own house in the expectation of finding a farm fairly quickly and we were about to be thrown out into the street. For an embarrassingly small difference we had sold a two and a half up, two down semi and had bought what was virtually two houses with about fifteen rooms between them. In addition, we had four acres of land and enough buildings to start a holiday camp.

We were well satisfied with our buy, especially when the dry rot proved to be a figment of the surveyor's imagination. The subsidence was shown to have taken place a hundred years previously and the house did not appear to have budged since.

We next had to move house. The removal men quoted prices that seemed a little excessive and so we decided to do it ourselves. I hired the largest van that my licence would allow and we stuffed in all our worldly goods. The van may have been a mini to a lorry driver but it was a tank as far as I was concerned. We moved during that week between Christmas and New Year which has recently been turned into a unilateral public holiday. I slalomed the lorry through the icy streets of the early rush hour and somehow achieved the M1 safely.

At about 10 am I decided that it was time for the first coffee break and took my foot off the accelerator to go into a service station. The truck ignored me and went trundling on. This was rebellion on the grand scale. I dabbed at the accelerator and nothing happened. The engine continued to roar flat out at 50 mph. I checked in the mirror and pulled on to the hard shoulder, switching off the engine. Nothing happened when I turned the key. The vehicle thundered on down the hard shoulder passing one or two disconcerted juggernauts on the inside. I was tempted to panic and jump out. The machine seemed to have taken over control. I pulled back on to the motorway, which seemed to please the brute as the engine note dropped slightly, and reached over for the handbook. '*This is a diesel truck*,' it informed me. The hirers must have been used to catering for idiots as the instructions were written in words of one syllable in large capitals. '*To stop engine. Pull knob marked Stop*.' A bit repetitive but clear enough.

I hunted along the dashboard and found no knob so marked and consulted the handbook once more. '*See diagram*' it said. The page with the diagram on it was missing. I pulled out all the knobs that I could find, demolishing a neat line of warning cones which popped out of the carriageway when my attention was distracted. I achieved nothing except the discovery that the window wipers did not work. The next service station was looming up, so I swerved down the entry road and roared into the car park. There I jammed on the brakes and put in the clutch. The engine, furious, tried to shake itself from its moorings. I waited until the van had stopped and let the clutch out with a jerk. The brute stalled and there was silence apart from the tinkle of broken crockery behind me.

A friendly lorry driver pointed out the stop knob, nestling beneath the driver's seat. Having got this far, I was damned if I would give up without a struggle. He and I traced the accelerator and found the vital bit that was faulty. The bloke on the end of the telephone told us that a replacement could be got to us within a fortnight. We rigged up a bit of string from the stop knob round the steering wheel to my teeth. This enabled me to slow down by pulling my head smartly back thus turning off the engine, leaving my hands free to juggle with the steering wheel, gears, indicators etc.

Eventually I arrived at the farm and roared twice round the yard after the string had snapped. I unloaded the furniture, swept the crockery into a plastic bag and set off back. Waterloo came at the stroke of midnight as the old year died. I had managed to negotiate the drunks of London without mishap and was only about 150 yards from the hirer's garage. By this time the indicators had also given up and I was just going through the complicated movements necessitated by a desire to slow down and turn right when a mini cab decided to pass me. I had not got a spare hand to wave at him through the window. He was unamused when I bounced him off a lamp post and stole his door.

Fortunately nobody was hurt. The company from which I had hired the van said that they had not bothered to service their vehicles as the whole fleet was to be changed the following day. They refused to give me a discount for the mental anguish they had put me through.

The following day, New Year's Day, we finally shook the dust of London off our feet and headed for the farm. It was snowing. The cat was in a filthy mood. There was the usual winter miners' strike in progress and we had no coal. To say the least, our new home was decidedly chilly. For the first week we lived in the kitchen - an enormous room with icy flagstones - surrounded by tea chests. Much of the day was spent huddled round the electric stove with its door open and all the hobs going full blast. At intervals one of us would unwrap him or herself from the blankets and sweep the snow back out under the door.

The main source of heat in the house was a solid-fuel stove which crouched in a corner of the kitchen and malevolently refused to allow itself to be lit. It eventually surrendered to half a gallon of paraffin being poured down its chimney and consented to fill the house with dense clouds of oily black smoke. I have yet to encounter one of these stoves that is anything other than a pain in the arse, but that one was exceptional. It used to go out several times a week which necessitated setting aside an afternoon for the attempt to coax it back to life. If it was in a particularly foul mood it would stealthily fill the house with carbon monoxide and try to murder us in our beds. A CO headache puts even a brandy headache to shame.

18

Eventually the snow began to melt; the wind ceased to whistle round our ankles and we found a coal merchant who was open to bribery. Things were looking up a bit.

Bringing Home the Bacon

When we put our noses round the corner of the blankets and surveyed the world we were faced by a bit of a problem - the small one of actually earning a living. Granted we had a house, a large quantity of buildings and a diploma, but the actual business of putting our ideas into practice was rather daunting. I really had not got a clue. I would not know a bad pig from a good pig. I had no idea how you went about buying them, selling them or feeding them. The one thing that the correspondence course had thoroughly drummed into my head was that scrupulous cleanliness was an essential part of being a successful pig farmer.

The previous occupants of the buildings had left their premises covered in a fine layer of cow dung, and so I happily set to cleaning it up in preparation for some pigs. It may sound a bit daft, but the Grand Design nearly fell apart at the first fence. It became quite obvious why certain primitive peoples built houses of dried animal dung. I scrubbed it, wiped it, hosed it but nothing very much seemed to happen. The solution seemed to be a knife and a very smelly wad of sandpaper combined with hours of laborious effort. Those Welsh cows had a most peculiar system of plumbing. The stuff was splattered all over the walls up to a height of about seven feet. There was one pen which even outdid the Maze Prison H blocks with the ceiling carefully coated as well. Eventually I gave up and bought some whitewash which was cheating but at least it looked good.

At about this time, we were discovered by the salesmen. There are at least five agricultural salesmen to every farmer and we were descended upon by droves of them. It was one of the penalties for being close to the main road. The essence of salesmanship is to persuade your boss that you are a grafter and easy calls right on the main road are the quickest way to fill up your daily sheet without putting yourself out too much.

I was a lovely juicy target. No commitments and a nice healthy overdraft waiting to be taken up. The word got round like news of a gold strike. We were visited by people selling drugs, brushes, hoses, tractors, meal, water bowls, fences, life insurance and even the odd one selling pigs. It was quite bewildering since, like all salesmen, each of them sold the very best product available on the market without which no pig farmer could ever hope to succeed. We did not know enough to be able to sort out one man's claim from another's and we looked like becoming bogged down in a morass of indecision.

They were useful, however, because before I would agree to sit down and listen to their spiels they had to agree to apply a bucket of whitewash to the dung-covered buildings. Quite a lot of work was done. The more who came to extol the benefits of their own particular products, the more reluctant I became to part with money for fear of making some ghastly mistake.

About two weeks after moving in, it became obvious that something would have to be done. We decided that I would have to find a job on somebody else's farm so that I could learn something about the practical side of pigs. Otherwise we would sink without a trace. I extracted the names of some of the local pig farmers from a friendly rep (I let him off whitewashing for the information), brushed up a bit of pig jargon to impress prospective employers and went visiting. The first name on the list was only a mile away. The rep's instructions about how to get there were quite clear. 'Turn left by the crematorium. Right at the first slag heap and then left at the second. Straight on past the rubbish tip and it's on your left.' I found it as easily as he had said I would. An immaculate tarmac entrance drive, white-painted fences and barns and not a pig in sight. I went up to the front door and knocked, nervously suspecting that I had come to the wrong place. There was no sight of any pig. A tall grey-haired man opened the door and I could tell by his smell that here, at last, was a real pig farmer.

'Yes?' he said.

'Good afternoon, my name is Robertson. I wonder if you

could help me?'

'I'm sorry. I don't want to buy anything today.' My admiration rose. What a delightfully simple, concise way of getting rid of reps. Just tell them to piss off. Why hadn't I thought of that?

'No, you don't quite understand. I'm not selling anything, I'm just after some advice.'

'Advice. What do you mean?'

'Well. Perhaps a bit more than advice. I've just bought the farm up the road, I want to keep pigs on it and I don't quite know how to start. I was told you were a pig farmer and I was hoping you might be willing to help me by, say, letting me work here for a few weeks, just so that I could find out which end of a pig is which.'

He looked at me rather suspiciously for a moment. 'You're going to be a pig farmer?'

'A pig breeder.'

'- a pig breeder and you haven't bought any pigs yet?'

'That's right.'

'Have you bought any equipment yet?'

'No.'

'Do you know much about pigs?'

'No.'

'And he doesn't know a damn thing about pigs.' A smile broke out over his face and he put a protective arm round my shoulders. 'Come in.' I allowed myself to be led into the kitchen. One shelf was lined with china pigs. My knees felt weak with emotion. His wife was seated at the table doing some accounts with a worried look on her face.

'Put the kettle on, dear,' he said. 'We've got a guest.' He turned to me. 'My name is Ted. You're.....?'

'James.'

'Jim. I'm delighted to meet you. Jim here is starting a pig farm up the road and he's come to us for some advice. He hasn't got a pig on his place yet and no equipment. He wants to know the best way to begin. Isn't that it, Jim?'

'Yes.' An expression of awed wonder stole over his wife's face, rather like that which must have been apparent on the faces of the shepherds when Gabriel dropped in for a chat and they realised that it was more than the local home brew at work. She gave me a beaming smile and started to stuff sticky cakes down my throat while humming the Hallelujah Chorus. I passed the rest of the afternoon being hospitalitied to death; Ted agreed to come out the following day to look around our farm and give us the benefit of his expertise.

Ted ran an immaculate set-up with fifty breeding sows. He had been in pigs for the past fifteen years and before that he had sold printing presses in the United States. He could understand what I was up against in trying to start a pig farm without any previous experience as he had done much the same sort of thing himself. Unfortunately, he was unable to offer me a job but, out of the kindness of his heart, he was willing to offer me as much help and advice as he could. He did not really think that it would be worthwhile to take a job somewhere else because all I would learn would be the varieties and textures that pig muck could achieve. It would be much better if I bought a few pigs myself and learnt on the spot with his help and guidance.

Ted came round and started to explain the best way we could lay out our buildings to house pigs. He was very firm with one or two meal reps who turned up when he was on the premises. They had schemes whereby the farmer could buy or lease pigs from them as long as he used their particular brand of feed. He advised me strongly to preserve my independence.

Ted invited me and my wife round to dinner and the wine, bottle after bottle, flowed free. When I was feeling the full effects, he turned the conversation round to pigs.

'It's very difficult to start in pigs,' he said.

I blearily agreed.

'The trouble is that most people start with gilts. It takes a long time before the first piglets arrive and the money starts flowing in.'

23

'I know, I know,' said I.

'You really want to have an instant working herd.'

'Yes. That would be ideal. But there's no chance of that.'

'......a herd rather like mine.'

'Yes. I really envy your set-up.'

'You envy my herd, you mean.'

'Yes, that's what I mean. You've got the ideal herd for me.' We all looked solemnly at our glasses while Ted refilled them. There was a short pause before he spoke again.

'I'm thinking of retiring, you know.'

'Really? What a shame.'

'It is. It will be such a shame to break up the herd. I mean we'd like to sell the stock intact to a good home, wouldn't we, dear?'

His wife looked a little uncomfortable. 'Yes, we would.'

It was then that I had a marvellous idea. 'Why don't you let me buy your herd?'

Ted gave a merry laugh. 'It's not that simple. We'll have to have an auction because we've got to sell all the equipment too.'

'Why don't you sell me all that as well?'

Ted and his wife looked at each other. 'Do you know,' said Ted, 'that might work.'

'Work? It would solve all your problems and solve all mine. It's an excellent idea.' I was quite a convincing salesman in those days. Over the next couple of hours we thrashed out all the details. Along with Ted's herd, I would also buy his expertise and he agreed to advise me on the solution to any problems that might arise until I had gained enough experience to deal with them myself. Ted sold his entire output to one fattener who bought the piglets at about 60lb or nine weeks old and I would take over that contract. Ted also bought his meal as part of a buying group which meant that he bought it cheap. I would take over his place in that.

It all made wonderful sense. As of the first of March I would buy his herd, his equipment and any meal that he should have left. Ted undertook to transport everything across to us as we prepared the buildings to house them. Meantime he would look after the stock for nothing until we were ready.

Our new source of income consisted of fifty-two Saddleback sows and three boars, two of which were Large White and one Saddleback. Part of my course had given me a rundown on the various breeds of pig, so I had some idea of what I was buying. Large Whites were large and white, but the sows were clumsy and could easily squash their young. Landrace were longish and Scandinavian, but tended to go lame. Saddlebacks made excellent mothers but got fat. Tamworths were ginger and pretty. The Duroc was American and therefore grew very fast but was of poor quality. The Pietrain tended to be dead. The combination of a Large White boar and a Saddleback sow produced the blue pig of fable - so called because it had the odd bluish blotch on its otherwise white skin. These piglets were beginning to go out of fashion as they tended to take after their mothers and put on fat rather than lean meat.

I was beginning to discover the criteria by which farmers judge their stock. It was completely different from that of the layman and I never really mastered it. The average man will look at a pig and say 'How sweet' or 'How hideous' according to individual taste. The farmer does not really see the animal at all. He will see a quantity of rashers of middle cut bacon; when it turns round there will be revealed some nice juicy chops and a brace of fine hams. It needs a detachment from the stock that we never really mastered. We owned some animals that had the ability to drive us insane with fury at times but we never owned a collection of sausages, chops and spare ribs.

We now had to prepare the cow buildings to house pigs. The first thing we concentrated on was accommodation for sows. We decided to group them together in yards. The alternative systems either required lots of acres for them to roam around in or for large chunks of capital to be invested in stalls in which they would be tied all day. We had not enough acres for free ranging and the idea of chaining the animals up all day was rather distasteful, quite apart from the fact that we were now deficient in capital following Ted's successful raid upon our overdraft. The sows were to live in half a dozen batches underneath the roof of a Dutch barn and in the old cow cubicle shed. All we had to do was split this into separate yards.

We bought some concrete blocks, some sand and cement and started to make mud pies. In those days I was turning my hand to all sorts of things that I had never tried before and this was one of them. I soon found that the art of building a straight, secure wall was not as easy as the experts made it appear. We found an odd-job man who was prepared to come and lend a hand at weekends and his were the only walls that were not full of subtle curves and sudden changes of level. I later discovered that walls on almost every farm were just about as bad as mine.

I have always been a great believer in a quick botch job as long as it serves its purpose. The fact that the majority of these walls looked as if they had been built by a drunk with a severe squint bothered neither the pigs nor myself. The method I employed was to pile the blocks on top of each other with a dab of mortar in between, wait until the mortar had dried and then give the wall a hefty shove to see if it would fall down. If it did, I would start again, but it was surprising how many stayed up..

The odd-job man would come along weighed down by spirit levels and plumb lines and spend much of his day trying to line up two or three blocks to his own satisfaction. Watching him I used to gloomily calculate how long it would take him to finish his wall and then work out the cost of his time. He used to become very annoyed if I completed one of his walls in my fashion between his visits, but otherwise we would never have been ready for our stock. We eventually completed four rather rickety-looking sow yards, and Ted prepared to unload some pigs on us.

The selected batch consisted of ten sows and a boar. The sows had just been weaned off from their litters straight into Ted's lorry. From careful study of the correspondence course I discovered that they were due to come on heat within three or four days when the boar should do his duty. The pen in which they were to live had been the old cowshed and still had rows of tubular metal cubicles stretching down either side. We had rigged up a gate at one end to keep them in and thrown some straw along one side to provide comfortable sleeping quarters. The gate was beside a water trough next to which, according to the book, the pigs would dung in a neat pile, allowing me to sweep the muck out without any difficulty. Apparently pigs liked to dung beside their water which sounded like one of evolution's lousier ideas, particularly if they happened to be desert-dwelling pigs.

Ted drove his lorry up to the cubicle shed and lowered the tailboard to unload. Up to this point the pigs had been a matter of academic discussion and theory. The sight of the actual animals themselves was something else. If you mix a number of pigs after a few weeks' separation - in this case the sows had been isolated with their litters for six weeks - add a boar and a new environment such as the lorry, the result is fairly chaotic as they try to sort out their pecking order. They were sceaming, roaring and fighting. Now a couple of tons of bellowing pig flesh trying to tear itself to pieces as it rolled in teeth-gnashing clusters down the ramp of the lorry is a fairly daunting spectacle; particularly since it was my job to love and cherish every pig until death did us part. I was forced to find a commanding view of the slag heaps and sit down to reflect on all the compensations of country living before I returned to face the inevitable death that contact with such animals would bring.

The pig is probably the most intelligent of the domestic animals and by far the most argumentative. Sheep are fully certified morons with a collective death wish. A cow always has a slightly dreamy air about it and looks as if its spring needs winding up. Its teeth have never scared anything larger than a blade of grass. Pigs, though, have the reactions of Björn Borg and sets of razor sharp, yellowing teeth to help them sort out life's little problems. As his helpers unloaded these brutes, Ted cheered me by telling me about a local pig farmer who was killed and half-eaten by his boar a few years back.

The sight of the sows was bad enough, but the boar was terrifying. A mature Large White boar, as was this, can weigh up to half a ton. He had a fine pair of curly tusks which were obviously a lot more than ornamental judging by the way that he was using them to sort out the sows. In addition to his bulk and his tusks, the other quite outstanding feature of the animal was the size of his testicles. Any Casanova is bound to feel desperately inadequate on his first close-up look at a boar.

Ted gravely advised me never to enter a pen with a boar unless I had a brush or a board with which to fend him off should he become frisky. I tried to look grateful for the information but I had no intention of getting into a pen with a sow, let alone a boar, without a heavily armed guard ready to lay down his life in my defence. Anyway Ted departed and left me alone with my first pigs. I had to ensure that they were fed, watered and that the sows were properly served by the boar. A careful note of the dates of service had to be taken to ensure that I would know when the future litters were due to be born.

The following morning - Day One in my life as a brand-new pig farmer - I donned my immaculate gumboots and went to meet destiny. Destiny, on peeking round the door, appeared to be sound asleep in the straw which suited me fine, and there was a large pile of muck in the middle of the floor. In the well-organised pig pen the concrete floors all slope in the same direction so that any muck and urine will wend its way gently towards the drain, thus obviating the need for much manual labour. In this pen, it flowed sweetly to the centre where it sat and fermented.

I tiptoed into the pen with my brush and prepared to remove it. There was a grunt and every pig leapt to its feet and charged at me. Rarely has man moved faster. With an Olympic-winning bound I was over the gate to safety leaving the pigs growling and squealing with rage at having failed to tear me limb from limb and crunching up my abandoned broom in their disappointment.

I got on the phone to Ted crying for care and protection, but for a man who was taking my money he was most unsympathetic. He said that they only wanted their food but, having seen the blood lust in their piggy little eyes, I was not entirely convinced. With considerable courage I returned to the scene, faced up to the furious squeals and tossed a bag of meal into the thickest part of the mob. Miraculously they turned their attention from me and started to fight each other for the food. While they were distracted, I hurriedly nipped over the gate and removed the worst of the muck.

Over the next few days my terror gradually abated to be replaced by acute mistrust and I became almost nonchalant about going over the top. The iron cubicles proved to be a blessing as I was able to take refuge behind one of them if a pig came too close and beat it off with a brush. The boar still managed to turn my knees to jelly. Apart from his sheer bulk and his tusks, he would polish off the lion's share of the food and then come after me, roaring, to demand more food while I was trying to remove the night soil. I became quite adept at hurdling the cubicles to keep ahead of him, holding the brush in one hand and a shovelful of hastily gathered muck in the other which I used to fend him off.

The sows spent their waking moments scrabbling over the food, dropping large piles of dung and indulging in a series of highly alarming running battles to establish a pecking order determining which of them had the choicest sleeping spots. The poor sow who was bottom had to sleep beside the water trough and she even grew to be afraid of me which did wonders for my morale.

Day Three came and went, but the boar showed no signs of wanting to do what came naturally. The course stated categorically that sows came on heat at Day Three after weaning and showed this by a reddening and swelling of the vulva and, rather bizarrely, would allow the farmer to sit on their backs. The relevance of this last piece of information escaped me at the time but experience taught me that, when a sow is good and ready, she will stand like a rock waiting for the boar to jump on her. My function was supposed to be to jump first just to check her stage of sexual readiness. After Days Four and Five we decided that the boar must have preferred privacy, and so we took to creeping up on him and peering through cracks to find out if he was yet performing his conjugal rights.

Finally, about five days after something should have happened, something did happen. One morning I found the boar boaring happily away on the back of Number Eleven. Almost immediately the other sows showed signs of coming on heat. At least I presumed that their habit of jumping on each other's back and generally playing doctor showed a degree of randiness consistent with heat. The trouble was that the boar appeared to be besotted by Number Eleven.

The book said that each sow should be served twice to ensure maximum litter numbers but it did not tell me how I was supposed to pass this information on to half a ton of lovesick boar. Eleven was served twice and then again and again. I thought of trying to pen her separately to give the other sows a chance but the boar seemed to think that I was some kind of sexual threat. If I got too close to his beloved he would come at me chomping his jaws in rage and splattering the surrounding area with foam. The other sows were obviously suffering from acute frustration but nothing would woo the boar, now christened George, from his one true love.

Matters reached a crisis after Number Eleven had had all the hair worn from her back by George's ministrations. I went into the cubicle shed one afternoon in response to squeals of anguish. The two of them had been trying an interesting new position and were inextricably tangled in the ironwork of one of the cubicle divisions. I had to chop it apart with a hacksaw before they were freed. After three days, Number Eleven went off heat which left George free to try his luck elsewhere but, by then, all the other sows had left their heat periods behind them. There were now one very thoroughly served sow and nine empties. As empties eat as much food as pregnant sows, this first attempt at pig breeding had proved rather disastrous. Something would have to be done next time round.

While this was going on Ted was continuing to dump pigs on us. His next batch was made up of five sows and their litters. We had decided to use the multi-suckling system which meant plonking the whole batch together rather than housing each litter individually. It was cheap and would require the minimum of alteration to the existing cow buildings in order to make it work. The other advantages of this system lay in early mixing of litters which reduced stress and fighting later on and cut out the need for duplication of facilities such as creeps. The main drawback was that instead of the feet of only one sow for the piglets to avoid, there were four or five and the young had to be pretty nimble on their pins to avoid being squashed. Another hazard was that the stronger pigs could start suckling from more than one sow to the detriment of whosoever's teat they might choose.

We set up a stable as our first multi-suckling unit. It could have been almost tailor-made for the job, having one large section and a nine-inch gap through to another smaller section where I set up an infra-red light to warm the straw for the nursery. Its only snag was the floor which was made up of what I believe are called stable bricks; they have nice deep grooves on them to allow the resident horse a good grip. They may or may not have been good for that, but they enabled the pig muck to take the most remarkable hold and many happy hours were needed to remove the stuff.

Ted's wagon lumbered into the yard for the second time. The five sows disembarked with the usual amount of noise, effort and inconvenience on every side, and every available helper gathered armfuls of small piglets and carried them in to unload them beside their mothers. They all seemed to settle down quite happily; Ted left me with instructions to keep a close eye on the colour and consistency of the piglets' dung and watch for any signs of crushing.

The first thing he failed to warn me of was the ear-shattering screaming noise that the piglets emitted as they fought for a teat on which to suckle. The first few times that they fed we would come down to investigate this awful noise, quite convinced that one of the sows had lost her marbles and was engaged in full-scale slaughter. This noise was something that we could never become used to. It would wake us up out of a deep sleep at 2 am and we would lie there, knowing that it was nothing more than the usual suckling noise. Then one scream would rise up over the others and persist. After a couple of minutes my nerve would crack and I would get up to rescue the beast which was obviously trapped under a sow. I would get there and find the screamer wandering about the pen in a fury because its teat had been pinched by somebody else. I would hurl half a brick at it and return to bed.

It was even worse those first few nights. To the screams of the piglets were added the screams of a badger. I have never heard the noise since but, apparently, at some stages of its courting procedure the badger can let out screams that would have put even King Kong off his stroke. The combination of the pigs and this badger kept us on the hop all night more effectively than a dose of syrup of figs.

In spite of almost 24 hour attendance we found our first dead piglet the morning after the sows arrived, lying in the main section of the pen. Undoubtedly it had been crushed. We took it round to the guru, Ted, who gravely examined it and agreed with my diagnosis. We brought the body home and buried it in a biscuit tin in a sunny part of the garden. During the rest of the day I kept a very close eye on the piglets but they all seemed quick on their feet and quite smart enough to keep out of the way of Mother.

We decided that the corpse must have been inhabited by a mental defective who was too stupid to realise that 400lb of pig is not the best thing to stay beneath as it flings its legs to the side and crashes down for a kip. I took my life in my hands to muck them out full of dark forebodings about mother love, but there were no grave difficulties.

We passed another sleepless night with much the same result - one more corpse. Ted gave his diagnosis once more and another biscuit tin was commandeered. The odd-job man then stuck in his oar. Like everyone else in the vicinity he kept a few pigs on the side and was therefore an expert worth listening to. He put it down to polywogs and straw. We were giving the pigs far too much straw for bedding. This was interfering weith the piglets' footwork and tripping them flat on their snouts when they were scampering out of the way.

The polywogs were rather more worrying. One of the difficulties he was up against as he tried to make perfection in mortar was the quality of our water. It was pumped about a hundred yards from a rather turgid stream which changed colour from a violent orange to green or blue depending what was being dumped in it further up. Below us it was always consistently brown as it had been used as the farm sewer for generations. The Water Board, in whose reservoir it ended up, did not seem to be too worried by this. We made quite sure that our own drinking water came from another source.

The water system could have provided useful employment for someone all day. It was not so much the length of the pipe that caused the trouble but the rise of about fifty feet from the stream to the farm. No doubt any self-respecting schoolboy can work out what the total weight of water contained in this pipe should be, but it was far too much for any non-return valve that I could fix to the inlet end of the pipe. When the water in the storage tank fell to a certain level, a fiendishly cunning float switch would turn on the pump which would emit a few gurgles and a faint fart and produce nothing but air.

Then the pump's employee would have to spend half an hour carefully filling the pipe with water as fast as he could to beat the dribbling emission at the other end. If he was lucky, the pipe would start ejaculating water in a spasmodic fashion and all would be well for an hour or two before the entire process would have to be repeated.

Aside from the sheer aggravation of actually getting any water, the odd-job man was upset by the strange colour it could attain and the creepy crawlies and the odd dung-eating minnow that turned up in his bucket. His contention was that the whole horrible brew was not only spoiling the smooth surface of his mud pies but was also having a deleterious effect on the digestion of the piglets. His argument seemed to make sense and so we decided to convert the buildings' water supply from the stream to the mains.

Our existing mains water which supplied the house came through a pipe which had been laid back in the dawn of time. It meandered its way between a couple of slag heaps and across several fields - about half a mile in all. Its line was easily followed by the necklace of bogs that marked its progress. There was about one hour in twenty four, between 4 and 5 am when the water pressure was high enough to counteract the leakage and water actually reached the house. We hired a man with a digger and he laid a new pipe which initially blew every valve on the farm and fractured half the rusting pipes when the water was first switched on.

With all this lovely clean water the piglets now had no excuse for anything but perfect health and the odd-job man's walls and concrete took on a new beauty. The pigs, however, continued to die. Soon there were five lining the rose bed and we were fast running out of biscuit tins. I carried one off-colour piglet round to Ted and the beast gently expired on his drawing room carpet. Even Ted had to agree that it would be hard to blame that particular death on the sow's big feet and the decision was made to call in the vet.

The vet grew to love and cherish me because my pigs provided him with a large proportion of his income. On this, his first visit, he diagnosed kidney failure brought on by some obscure bug that had belonged to the horse which had been the previous inhabitant of the pen. He gave us a large bottle of antibiotics with instructions to inject each piglet daily for three days. That was easier said than done. You first of all separate the sows from the piglets to prevent your leg being bitten off by the irate mother when her young starts to scream as the needle enters its wriggling leg. Then when half of them have been speared, the sow knocks over the partition that divides them and the little pigs pile up in a great heap in the corner for mutual protection. That is the point at which you give up as you have no idea which pigs have been stabbed and which have still to be done. One of the big problems with managing little pigs is that all the little sods look exactly the same.

Easy as (Pork) Pie?

During my attempts to grow to love the pigs, my wife had been trying to set the house in order. From living in the kitchen we had been gradually spreading to other parts of the house. One of the first things we did was to knock down the partitions that had prevented the evacuees from cohabiting. We carefully dismantled them and re-erected them in the yards to see if they would keep the pigs apart. It gave them a couple of days' amusement while they tore them to bits.

The house was divided into two - the smaller section had been used as a farm worker's cottage. Certain things needed putting right as a matter of urgency. The woodworm in the roof were given a very hard time by an expert who disappeared into the loft for a couple of days before re-emerging with an enormous bill in his hand. He was followed by another expert who stopped up the worst of the leaks.

With the aim of producing an additional income, we filled up the annex with furniture salvaged from the local auction rooms and let it out. The Rents Acts, then, were not quite as formidable as they later became. Even so there was a certain amount of doubt whether we would be able to get a tenant out once he had moved in. We decided to use an estate agent to find us a nice clean respectable individual who would not give us trouble. The agent found us Bernie.

Bernie was about thirty and exceedingly short. He had, in great abundance, that ghastly brand of cocksureness that is most often seen in young Conservative MPs just after their first winning election. When we were introduced he pumped my arm effusively, clasping both his hands around mine. He had a navy blue blazer with brass anchor buttons and an enormous embroidered coat of arms on the breast pocket with a Latin motto. This was worn with a striped cravat.

He was supposed to pay the rent money each Friday, but it never worked out like that. Every Monday I would have to go over to pay him a call. It was not much of a trip - straight across the washing green and a quick tap on his door. Bernie would open it in his dressing gown, at least up until 3 pm when he would sometimes be clothed. He would have a cigarette in a long holder and a brace of nubile damsels lurking in the background.

'Ah James, come in for a cup of coffee. We're just putting on the kettle. Or would you prefer something a little stronger?'

'No thanks, Bernie. I'm just calling for the rent.'

'Ah yes.....the rent. Isn't it due on Friday?'

'Yes Bernie. It's due on Friday.'

'But today is Monday.'

'Today is Monday. But you didn't pay last Friday.'

'Good Lord. Are you sure?'

'Yes Bernie, I'm sure.'

'I am most frightfully sorry. Here let me introduce you to the girls. Sharon, Yvonne. Come and meet my blood-sucking land-lord.'

Sharon and Yvonne would come giggling forward and Bernie would put a protective arm round each of them as he introduced them, looking like a down-market version of Noel Coward.

'The girls and I are off to the races this afternoon. Aren't we ladies?'

'Yes, Bernie,' they would chorus.

'These two can spot a good ride a mile off. Eh?' This would be accompanied by a series of galvanic winks at me while the girls would dissolve into giggles. I could never work out where Bernie managed to come across such a chicken-brained selection of women as were his usual choice.

'Are you sure you won't come in for a drink?'

'Quite sure thank you, Bernie,' I would reply.

'Well, if you'll excuse us, we'd better start getting ready. Isn't that right, girls?' They would start giggling again.

'The rent, Bernie.'

'Good Lord yes, the rent. I almost forgot. I'm just a little bit short at the moment. Could you come back on Friday?'

'Sorry Bernie.'

'Oh.' He'd pause for thought. 'Hang on a minute.' He'd disappear and leave the girls and myself staring at each other and then re-emerge with a bloody plastic bag containing 20lb or so of beef. 'How about taking this in lieu of rent this week?' I would make a quick calculation in my head and find out that it was worthwhile. At any rate, it would make a change from the eternal casualty pigs that were the usual inhabitants of our deep freeze.

'Where did you get this from, Bernie?'

He would tap the side of his nose, confidentially. 'Ask me no questions and I'll tell you no lies. Just came from a friend.'

'OK, Bernie. It'll do for this week, but I'll want cash on Friday.'

'Of course, of course. It's just that I thought you might prefer some beef. Excellent quality, I assure you. Aberdeen Angus, you know.'

It was not always beef. If I was engaged in building work, it would be bags of cement blocks. He even tried to palm off a colour television in exchange for a couple of free months. The estate agent telephoned us, full of apologies, about a week after Bernie had moved in. He had only just found out that Bernie had a Record. He had been a Wrong Doer. However, he assured us that Bernie's Debt to Society had been paid and he was quite sure that we would have no trouble. He was sure that we agreed that it was our duty to help those less fortunate than ourselves.

Bernie suited us fine. He stayed in the cottage for about eighteen months. During his final three months he got a job servicing fruit machines and then disappeared with the company car and half the takings. For a few months after that we had a series of visits from disconsolate debt collectors and HP men. The only damage that Bernie ever did us was that he ruined my local credit rating. He had passed the word round the district that he owned the farm and employed me to keep his pigs for him. After he had gone, I had great difficulty in persuading the local suppliers otherwise and getting any goods on tick. Last time I heard of Bernie he had won a prize for making a model of Chester Cathedral out of matchsticks during a sojourn in Winson Green.

One of Bernie's greatest coups was coming up with a truck-load of polystyrene sheets. Over the course of our time on the farm they were used all over the place as insulation for floors, walls and roofs. The first batch was used to create a false roof in the building that we had designated as the farrowing house. Pig farming is a constant battle to keep your charges warm. If you don't, they eat more food or get annoyed and die on you.

To help me erect this roof I roped in a couple of brothers who had come visiting for the weekend. We had our routine with visitors. In the morning they would go for a nice country walk with the dog. The route passed up the lane that wound its way along the banks of the stream, usually a pale pink at weekends, and then round the slag heaps where mangy, dysentery-ridden cattle would pick for feed amid the rock and clinker. Then there was a path leading across some fairly decent fields where the district's concentration of wildlife could find their only unpolluted living space. The guests would hit the main road through the industrial estate before branching up the country lane lined on one side by bungalows with the crematorium at the top and with our farm standing on a hillock on the other.

They would be allowed some lunch when I would fill them full of alcohol so that they would settle quite happily down to work in the afternoon, knowing that they had fully explored the beauties of rural Wales. We found that there were two types of visitor; those who retired into a corner with their stomachs heaving at their first whiff of a shovelful of pigshit, and those who could think of infinitely better ways of running the enterprise and retired rather huffily to their offices if we did not slavishly follow their advice.

My brothers definitely saw themselves as experts. One brother was convinced that the best way to build the roof was to glue all the sheets together and then jam them up. He spent a happy afternoon trying to puzzle out why the sheets dissolved when he put glue on them. The other brother decided that the only sensible method was to suspend the sheets from pieces of string. He was on whisky rather than beer. Having tried and failed to gain acceptance as the foreman, I left them to it and, being the only practical handyman present, I set about building a wooden framework on which to nail the polystyrene. My trellis collapsed at about the time the string-suspending brother fell off his ladder and nearly hanged himself. Defeated, we retired back to the whisky bottle and watched the sun set over the distant scrap yard.

Different guests had different idiosyncrasies. One dear old soul had a passion for cleanliness and would spend hours scrubbing and disinfecting one particular square yard of concrete while the pigs shat all around him. Another had to be restrained when, after he had carefully cleaned out a pen, I reintroduced the pigs and they dared muck in it. One of the more satisfactory occasions was when a visitor of the retching variety decided to help muck out a pen, using my smart new pressure washer which he thought looked rather fun to operate. He pointed it into a particularly dungy corner and pressed the start button. A full half-gallon of well-matured pig muck caught him right between the eyes and so far as work was concerned he was a write-off for the rest of the weekend.

Ted was still shovelling pigs at us as fast as we could prepare the buildings for them. After the sows and litters, he brought sixty-seven piglets which had just been weaned from their mothers. They were small enough for me to feel safe in their company. They went into one of the many stables and thrived. These animals provided me with another source of income: I would bet any guest, at large odds, that they would be unable to stand motionless inside a pen of store pigs for more than a minute. The sucker would look at the terror-filled eyes of the pigs piled up in a corner and decide that it was a doddle. He would climb in and the piglets would peel themselves off the wall and come over to start chewing. I only lost once and the winner's gumboots, which I had lent him, were gnawed to ribbons. I took the money back to pay for the boots but gave him a plaster for his toe.

With these stores came our first sow ready for farrowing and a spare crate in which to house her. Being safely shut up inside her cage, she was the first adult pig whom I got to know with any degree of intimacy. We built a wall of straw bales round her to contain her expected offspring and suspended an infra-red bulb over one corner to keep them warm. We then sat back and waited for her to produce her pigs. Days passed and nothing happened. Both my wife and I decided that we would have to do something to amuse her as it must have been immeasurably tedious for her to be shut up in the crate all day. Her only break from her porcine thoughts was her daily feed and her twice-daily water bucket which I would plump down in front of her nose.

We gave her a football to play with hoping that she could bash it about to her heart's content and it would be too large to slip through the bars of the crate. It lasted an hour before she punctured and ate it. Her next toy was a chain which we hung above her head. This was a bit more successful. She spent her day biting and running it through her teeth which produced a sound more disturbing than chalk squeaking on a blackboard. We also gave her a transistor radio so that she had Tony Blackburn blathering away in her ear for much of the time which may have been a bit of an insult to her intelligence. At least three times a day I would visit her and tug away at her teats. The good book had told me that farrowing would be imminent when her milk started to flow.

In spite of my ministrations she dropped her litter between the 10 pm and 6 am tweaks. The final piglet was born in a heap of afterbirth and was dead when I went in and found them in the morning. Ted had both Large White and a Saddleback boar and, among the charms of this litter, were two purebred Saddlebacks along with seven crossbreds. It could be said to prove the efficacy of the double service or merely that the Large White's semen won a rather nasty race riot during the voyage up to the uterus.

I consulted the lecture in my course entitled 'Things to Do to Newborn Piglets' and leapt into action. First I had to hack off their teeth, apparently to prevent them eating the sow's teats. This was another curious evolutionary aberration like dunging by their water supply. I grabbed myself a pair of pliers, picked up my first pig and tucked it under my arm. The animal opened its mouth and let out a piercing shriek. I didn't blame the poor little sod. With the decibels washing over my face in pulsating waves I peered down its throat. Yes, there were certainly two nasty sharp looking teeth in each jaw. I took aim with the pliers and approached the animal's mouth.It promptly shut it. I stuffed my finger in to prise it open and got a decidedly old-fashioned look before it clamped those nasty looking teeth. They were very sharp indeed. My natural reaction to pain is 'Ow' followed by a revenging bash at the source, but smashing a newborn piglet on the skull seemed to be rather self-defeating, as my job was supposed to be keeping the pigs alive and healthy.

I dug out my wife. She held the pig while I carefully prised open the jaw and eventually clipped the teeth with one of those chalk-squealing crunches. It took about ten minutes per piglet.

It was some of the easiest and most obvious aspects of pig husbandry that gave me the worst problems. Take, for example, the simple process of administering injectable iron to prevent piglet anaemia. To give the beast its iron, you have to inject it in the buttock. A piglet-sized needle should be placed on the end of a syringe, inserted in the bottle of iron and the plunger withdrawn, thus sucking the iron into the syringe. That seemed straightforward enough, but the iron had the consistency of treacle and refused to flow as required.

After about 5 minutes' work the bottle eventually secreted enough of its contents to provide an acceptable dose and I selected a piglet, inserted the needle and depressed the plunger. The plunger refused to depress. Of course, if the stuff did not want to go in, it was equally unlikely to be willing to come out. Exerting all my strength, I pressed down on the syringe. The needle separated from its neck and a jet of liquid iron at high pressure smashed into my face. I then had to go into the house to wash the stuff off, sending my wife into hysterics at the sight of all this gore apparently dripping from my eye.

After cleaning up, I returned to the fray and discovered that I'd forgotten which of the little pigs had been done. I next found that the iron was even more difficult to suck out of its bottle and some minutes passed before I worked out that it was due to a vacuum building up inside. More minutes passed before I worked out how to get rid of it. The next piglet to be treated received the needle straight into the bone or the tendon. It let out a screech that sent the foraging rats scurrying for shelter on the nearby slag heaps. The sow went berserk in her crate and clamped her teeth round the heel of my gumboot and I dropped the piglet. And so it went on.

In spite of all this, that first litter gave us considerable pleasure. Within a week, after, according to my diagnosis, having been through every disease known to science they were thoroughly exploring the creep, playing tag over the top of the straw bales and chasing mice throughout the rest of the farrowing shed. There was one simple soul who would squeeze his way between the bales and not have the sense to back out. He would need to be rescued several times a day. Once I heard the screams that signified squashing and found this little beast standing up with the top of his head pressed against the lowest bar of the crate. He really thought that he was stuck as he could not lift his head any higher. A gentle push sent him on his way, grunting with relief at his narrow escape from untimely death.

While this litter was gaining in health and strength, Ted was still bringing over pigs and equipment. He brought over all the remaining crates as he weaned off the batch of sows at his end. We set them up, five on each side of the farrowing house in two neat lines. I bought some concrete blocks and dispensed with straw bales, building instead neat little walls to separate the crates from each other and provide individual creeps for each litter. There were three doors to this shed, which had been an old abreast milking parlour and these we hung with ancient Persian carpets, scavenged from one of the rubbish dumps. They acted as highly efficient draught excluders as well as providing a touch of the exotic. It added up to a superb farrowing house which, owing to the thickness of the walls in the 150-year-old barn in which it was contained, never varied more than a couple of degrees either side of 65°F day or night.

Ted had by now brought almost all the pigs over to us and he helped us move the ten heavily pregnant sows from the yard into the farrowing house where they settled down quite comfortably. They were all supposed to be producing litters within the week and busied themselves in building nests out of the straw bedding and generally remodelling their quarters to suit themselves. It had never occurred to me that the sows would be interested in poking their noses out of the crates to investigate the world beyond. This lot did and came up against my neat little walls. What added to the interest was that we had electricians in the farrowing house installing the wiring for infra-red lights and they were using the walls as step ladders. A snout would come out, nuzzle thoughtfully at one of the shoes and then give the walls a hefty shove to send the electrician tumbling. I hurriedly tried to fill the great gaping holes in the walls with some lengths of timber which kept the litters from being mixed up in the first few days.

The first of this batch farrowed when I was out. One of the electricians acted as midwife and was more excited than the mother. He was a lovely man whose total and consuming passion was tropical fish. He was the proud father of twelve excellent little pigs and kept a benevolent eye on them for the next couple of months, dropping in for a visit if he was in the area.

All these sows farrowed within three days of each other and had 105 piglets between them. We started off by neatly balancing the litters so that each sow had 10.5 young apiece. We need not have bothered. Within a week the piglets were hopping over the separating partitions and we took them down. It became chaotic, but the piglets thrived. They would all sleep under one of the creep lights in an enormous quivering mound. As soon as any sow made as to suckle, the mound would flow over her and she would be buried under a squealing, twitching heap of piglets that would drive her to her feet, snorting with alarm and scattering piglets like confetti from her flanks. Peace was only established on the occasions that all the sows decided to suckle at the same time.

All in all, it was a trouble-free batch. There were odd alarms and excursions - one piglet was sat on and joined its fellow martyrs in the rose bed - but we were beginning to think that raising pigs looked like being much easier than we had first thought. The sows themselves showed remarkable initiative in being able to prove troublesome with the very limited means at their disposal.

It is a truism to state that pigs like their grub but the sheer slavering delight of the pigs when they thought that feeding time had come round again was a constant source of rather uneasy wonder. I fed them in buckets in their crates each morning. When I came into the shed, they would all leap up and lean on the top of their crates and start squealing, making the air vibrate with their longing. One of them used to turn a complete somersault inside her crate every single morning which was extremely annoying as it meant leading her out of her crate and then back inside the right way round. I discovered that when her food was placed at her rear end, she managed another smooth back flip to get at it.

Apart from food, the other popular occupation of the sows was that of ripping the wooden floors of their crates to pieces. I was advised to cover the floors with tin to prevent this happening but found that this merely gave them pause for an extra day and all the ragged metal edges led to cuts in the piglets. They had fun with their water. Three times a day I would plonk a bucket of water in front of their noses and let them drink their fill. It was a highly inefficient system but undoubtedly cheap on capital

45

employed. It allowed me to have a good look at the piglets and check for any signs of ill health several times a day.

I had four or five buckets on the go at once. In theory, by the time that the last sow had received her bucket the first would have finished and her bucket could be passed on. The sows would race to drink their fill so that they could upset their buckets and make a lovely mess before I could get back to them. The system called for some pretty nimble footwork and was rather like a hurdle race as I hopped over pigs and walls to get to the sows who had finished before they could start playing about. One disadvantage of this system was that it proved rather expensive on creep bulbs. With all the rushing about, water would not infrequently splash on a bulb resulting in a loud bang as it exploded. This made every animal in the farrowing house, including me, leap in terror, after which there would be a deathly silence.

Another major snag in the smooth running of my water round was one of the sows who had never learnt to drink properly. She was convinced that water was a rather liquid form of meal which must be carefully chewed thirty-two times before swallowing to prevent indigestion. She would take three times as long as any other pig to drink her fill, and since I had to check on her progress at frequent intervals, this gave the other sows valuable seconds in which to spill their water.

POO!

With the pigs all stashed away in odd corners of the yard we turned our attention a bit more to the house, putting it gradually in order and tidying it up. We knocked out old fireplaces and discovered inglenooks behind them. We put four windows into a blank gable end and found four older windows that had been blocked up, presumably to avoid paying window tax.

The house was a mixture of buildings and styles. Trying to trace its history and that of the people who had lived there made a pleasant diversion from the pigs. The earliest reference we found was 1611 when it was inhabited by a widow and her eleven daughters. After this brood had left, the farm was bought by a London merchant who had made good and was in the process of turning himself into a landed gent. He let the land, used the house as the headquarters of his coalmining operations and began the process of turning the surrounding countryside into the maze of coal tips from which it is only now beginning to recover.

The merchant himself went bust, which served him right, and was forced to sell the estate to another Londoner; from the papers of his estate it has been possible to trace the ups and downs of the various tenants who worked the farm and lived in the house. There was the misfortune of one John Morgan, who got behind with his rent and was eventually evicted. He fell into acrimonious dispute with his landlord about how much money was owing. The landlord said that it was £111 and Morgan said £15. In 1716, the agent wrote in the rent roll, 'He insists that he was only half a year in arrears when he went off. And that Mr Green had produced fifteen measures of wheat which was sowed by Morgan. And his dung. And the hedging (2/8d).'

The Big House started to go downhill at about the turn of this century. The squire, when I was investigating, was the last of the line, a life-long bachelor who lived alone in his enormous dilapidated stately home which was waging a losing war against damp, rot and the subsidence caused by the coal mines which had originally made it rich. I used to go round there and root amongst the estate papers, surfacing at lunchtime when he and I would sit down to enjoy a glass of Madeira and a fish finger apiece.

This old man must have been the last of the true blue English eccentrics. Throughout his crumbling home there were piles of plates, filled with half-eaten cornflakes. If a thought struck him in the middle of breakfast he would pick up his bowl and paddle off to the source of interest. With him would go his ancient fox terrier, one side of which was scorched brown as it would always lie too close to the fire. When he arrived at his destination he would put his plate down and forget all about it. Once a month there would be a general collection when all the crockery would be returned to the kitchen to be scraped down ready for redistribution.

The house was crammed full of treasures, many of which were in an advanced state of decay. In one of the main bedrooms was a superb eighteenth-century four-poster bed. Above it, the roof had given up the unequal struggle and sagged so that all that kept it from crashing down was one of the posts of the bed. Through the roof the rain would pour, to be collected by a ring of buckets round the base of the post.

The garden had gone the same way as the house and was only kept in check by three hand-tame sheep which were used as automatic grass trimmers. When it rained these sheep came into the gallery that stretched the length of the rear of the house and were served tea in antique Chinese porcelain bowls. Remarkably, they appeared to be generally continent indoors but one had disgraced itself by charging its reflection in an enromous gilt-wood framed mirror that stood at one end, and had shattered it.

The charm of this house, now taken over by the National Trust, lay in its owner and the fact that the family had never thrown anything away. They hadn't repaired much either. Toys, bicycles, cars, furniture; anything that had come into the house had been carefully stored away once its usefulness had ended. Upholstery would be hanging in shreds from Chippendale chairs and bats would be roosting above the curtains but everything was there and in its original coverings. There was a splendid Victorian collection of oddments - shells from the South Seas, shrunken heads, strange insects. On this the ceiling had collapsed, shattering the glass cases and filling them with rubble and plaster.

In the huge cupboard where lay the estate papers I was continually having to evict the descendants of the generations of mice which had nested among the documents. Some of those which had not been chewed up to make nest linings presented a fascinating picture of life a few hundred years ago. There was the Squire's annual accounts of 1636. He had a house on old London Bridge where he kept an extremely rapacious mistress called Moll. Moll received a continual stream of presents, which culminated in the entry on St Valentine's Day, 'To my Moll. £6 and 2 yards of red ribbon.' His other big expense was boots and gunpowder which he consumed in inordinate quantities. He was stocking up for the Civil War.

I came across the journal of a son of the household for 1716, consisting mainly of his lewd thoughts and fantasies. It was not the sort of document that you would expect to find preserved among such papers and demonstrated that some of the pithier Anglo Saxon crudities which are normally inscribed on lavatory walls were alive and flourishing at the beginning of the eighteenth century.

There was a ritual about my visits which culminated in the Measurement of Subsidence. The Squire was always hoping for a large sum of money from the Coal Board in compensation for the gradual sinking of his house. His weekly duty was to monitor the amount that it had sunk over the previous seven days. He would hand me a striped surveyor's pole and send me to one end of the façade of the house while he hurled himself on his stomach at the other from where he would peer at me over his upraised thumb and start shouting instructions.

'Back a bit.... No, too far...A little to the left. There, that's it.

Stop.' I would stand there like a lollipop man while he lined up the tip of the pole with his thumb. 'Heavens,' he would yell. 'The west wing has sunk six inches in a week.'

'You're not lying in the same place as you were last time,' I would shout back.

'I don't see that it makes any difference.'

'But you're on a hump.'

'I don't understand.'

'Well, if you are six inches higher, I would think that the house is bound to look as if it is six inches lower.'

There would follow a short pause while he raised himself on his elbows and did some calculations in his notebook. 'Yes, that's quite possible, I suppose. I'll move over.' He would rise and dust himself down and choose another spot. 'This is much better. It's raised an inch.'

'That's impossible. Are you sure your thumb is straight?'

'Yes. Look.' He would wave his thumb in the air. It would look straight enough. 'How far have you dug the end of the pole into the ground?' He would ask.

'I'm resting it on top.'

'Well dig it in a bit. It's got a spike on the end. Use it.'

'But I always just rest it on top.'

'No you don't. Go on stick it in. I'm trying to align the tip with the top of that window behind you.' I would do as I was told and the final result that would be entered in the notebook for future civil action would be a seven-day rise of nine inches. The poor house seemed to go up and down like a yo-yo. Then we would retire back to the kitchen for a few more glasses of wine and I would eventually reel my way back across the fields between the slag heaps to my wife and the pigs to breathe Madeira fumes over them.

Back in the farmyard we were still trying to sort ourselves out and decide which pigs should go in which buildings. One thing we were not short of was advice. Apart from Ted, the odd-job man, the milkman and the lady who delivered the bread, all of whom kept pigs and gave me conflicting views, we received a constant stream of professional advisers. It was already becoming fashionable for salesmen to stop calling themselves salesmen and call themselves advisers instead. The meal firms were the worst sinners in this respect. They would have some wonderful system that depended for its success on using their own brand of meal.

One expert came to us from the Ministry of Agriculture to tell us how to get hold of the 40 per cent grant that they gave out in those days to help you doll up your farm. He was young but quite decisive. In order to receive the grant it was necessary to show that you were capable of earning something like £400 per annum and, with the greatest respect, he did not think that I had a hope in hell. So much for sweet dreams of £15,000 a year and no work.

One of the most awe-inspiring figures came from a similar government body and knew his job backwards. He was trying to advise me about the buildings. We suffered a complete breakdown in communication as I had not the faintest idea what he was talking about. He left us subtle plans covered in complicated equations relating to coefficients of expansion, thermal units and a baffling new world of aggregates and bedding which was somehow connected to the underside of concrete. I was under the impression that you just sloshed the stuff down and waited until it went hard.

He left us one piece of advice that we could understand and implement - that of feeding the sows in batches. Among the items of equipment that Ted had brought over had been a block of ten individual pens for feeding the sows. They sat in repainted tubular splendour in the middle of the yard and the original idea had been to buy sufficient of them to enable us to feed all the sows at once. That had been before Ted had stuck his claws into our bank account.

Without using the feeders the victualling of the sows consisted of skipping over the pen wall carrying a bag of meal and scattering it about, keeping a short trouser thickness ahead of the ravening swine. This was never satisfactory as the boars and the boss sows would guzzle most of it and the less dynamic and positive beasts would become thinner and thinner. Added to this was the problem of cleaning out the pens. While the pigs were busy eating, I would try to snatch all the dung I could. Then they would finish the meal and come trotting over to demand some more and drive me back over the wall to safety. There would be a gradual build-up of muck - particularly in the boar pens - as I never had time to clear away the previous day's offering.

With the new system, we put the feeders beside the sow yards and then released the pigs, pen by pen, to eat. With strict lack of favouritism I would rotate the order of being fed as it clearly meant a lot to the animals to be first in the queue. Most pig farms have a simultaneous or semi-simultaneous feeding system which enables a degree of silence to be maintained for all but a few minutes of each day.

Our feeding squeal would last for a couple of hours and in the mornings the neighbours down in the bungalows - a good three hundred yards away - would make angry telephone calls if I was late in starting and failed to waken them. The crematorium and the local garage used the hush that fell over the neighbourhood when the last pig was fed as a signal for their morning tea break. Most of the sow yard was covered by the curved corrugated iron roof of the Dutch barn which acted as a megaphone for every sound made on the farm. This could be a bit embarrassing, as my language tended to flow freely if I received a chunk of muck in the teeth, or something similar. My wife was walking past the crematorium four hundred yards away once and told me that she could hear every disgusting word I said.

This system made mucking out very easy as I had the pen to myself whilst its occupants were munching away in the feeders, oblivious of the agonised envy of all the other pigs. The feeders had other bonuses. It made examination of the individual sows simpler and we could teat tug or inject at leisure. However they did lead to a general rise in tension throughout those who were not actually being fed and it was rather unnerving to have my every move watched by pens of slavering sows, all willing me to open their gates and let them to the feeders. The gates themselves suffered and gradually became festooned with yards of barbed wire as I repaired the damage caused by the sows in their attempts to chew their way out.

The actual opening of one of these gates was a moment fraught with peril. The sows would be aware that it was coming round to their turn and they would be lined up by the gate with the decibel count and the excitement rising by the second. I would open the catch and the gate would be ripped from my hands as the wall of pig flesh exploded through the opening - woe betide me if I was not quick on my feet. Most of the pens were situated so that the animals had to negotiate a right-angle corner on their way to the feeders and there would be a frantic scrabbling of hooves as they tried to retain traction at the change of direction whilst travelling at 20 odd mph. There were some spectacular motorway-type pile-ups when one slipped and brought down the lot. Once I opened the gate and seven sows got stuck in a neat line in the opening with the laggards screaming in fury behind them. On that occasion the wall collapsed under the pressure.

My main preoccupation at this stage was dung. I found the quantity that a pen of mature animals could produce quite awe-inspiring. I began with a shovel, a brush and a wheelbarrow and soon became fed up. A sensibly organised pig farm is strewn with deep mysterious tanks that lap with evil-smelling liquids that change colour as the light catches them. These are sucked out every few weeks by stout-hearted machines manned by operators with heavy colds. I had to go over each pen with a brush daily.

Other people's pigs always seem to dung in neat barrow-sized piles beside the gate. Mine, when they were not playfully throwing it at each other, spread it tastefully over every inch of the surface or in the water troughs. The real experts placed it in inaccessible corners, requiring me to go in on hands and knees to retrieve it. Another speciality was to deposit it in my few existing drains, requiring an arm to fish deep down them to clear the obsrtuction.

Fortunately, the man who had dug our new water main had taken possession of a dumper in order to settle a debt and he accepted twenty pounds for it. For the expert, it was made by a firm called Fowler who, I was told, had gone out of business during the fifties. Ours, I suspect, had been one of their early experimental models. The only thing that held it together was dung which coated it with a grip much superior to Evostick. The astonishing thing about it was that it would go. It took some starting. Before I discovered the advantages of canned ether as a starting agent, I would flog away at the handle for upwards of fifteen minutes before it would eventually erupt in clouds of black smoke that rolled and billowed their way across to the coughing pigs. The smoke and a curious metallic clanging sound were its operational condition.

When it became bored it would shoot out spectacular clouds of sparks from its exhaust and once it set fire to a bale of straw sitting in the skip. Where it was not made of rust, it was made of old bedsprings which carried out various fundamental mechanical functions; these would drop off every few weeks and I would scout the local beauty spots for replacements.

In spite of its idiosyncrasies, it served its main shit-carrying function admirably. I would clank my way into the various pens and load it up with goodies and then gingerly conduct it towards the midden trying not to slop all over the yard. In winter, I would drop the skip and use it as a snowplough and, between these duties, it would drag a meal-laden trailer to all points of the farmyard.

Two of the pens had passages leading to them that were too narrow to be negotiated by the dumper. Just over the walls of these pens was a very convenient bank that fell fifty feet towards the road, and the dung from these pens used to end up being tossed over the walls and out of sight. I once had a rather alarming visit from an official of the water authority who sloshed his way through the slurry at the bottom of this bank to make sure that nothing untoward was getting across the road and into his stream. At one point he stood on the manhole covering the entrance to the sewer that took all the muck to his reservoir, but it was autumn, the cover was carpeted by fallen leaves and I was certainly not going to point it out to him.

It took about nine months to find a means of disposing of our dung and, by that time, the midden had become a masterpiece of manurial design, rivalling even the surrounding slag heaps. I had let one end of it harden and settle to form a ramp up which I would chug on the dumper to drop the skip at the top. At one point it looked dangerously as if it would take on a life of its own and amble ponderously down the hill, taking fences and trees with it before swallowing up one or two of the roadside bungalows. Just before this mucky Aberfan we found a neighbour whose fields were crying out for dung and, from then on, he removed it almost before it had time to leave the pigs. The stench of that first clearance was awesome. It took two weeks to get rid of the midden, and even the pigs thought about going off their food when its full power first wafted over their pens, peeling paint and rotting timber.

The old dumper eventually coughed its last, but not before giving me an intimate knowledge of the compression ignition engine that should stand me in good stead for the rest of my life. It passed peacefully away in its sleep. One morning it just would not start. I tied a rope from its axle to the bumper of the car to give it a pull start. When I let out the clutch of the car the axle on the dumper snapped in two and the machine sagged to the ground in a puff of rust. I received a £25 trade-in on a racy newish model - a garish yellow and scarlet with floral transfers stuck all over it to tart it up even further. It worked beautifully but lacked the character of its predecessor.

We made one other concession to the cause of modern mechanised farming when we bought a pressure washer. Cleaning out pens is the pig farmer's displacement activity. When life gets him down, his wife starts beating him or the pigs start to die on him through sheer spite, then he can go and relax by mucking out a pen. It is always a soothing, solitary, useful occupation. Using a pressure washer makes it even more relaxing. The whirr of the machine blots out the rest of the world as it cuts through the accumulation of shit and grime to the bare concrete below. Sometimes it even cuts through the bare concrete and rips it out in great chunks and tosses it aside. They are very expensive but can also be used for repelling pigs, watering the garden and putting out fires. One particular boar found it the sexiest thing in the world if I gave him a quick burst up the arse.

Sick as a Pig

Our second generation of piglets proved the fallibility of some of our farrowing dates. We had six sows in the batch due next and we moved them to the farrowing house and settled down to wait for our means of livelihood's miraculous appearance at their back-ends. One always had to keep a vague eye on the rest of the sows to make sure that none of them showed signs of farrowing out of turn but, one morning, I released a pen of ten sows and a boar to the feeders and noticed that there was one short. She was lying at the back of the pen in labour with nine piglets milling vaguely round her.

One of her litter had already been squashed which was hardly surprising with forty-odd trotters trampling about. I whipped the sow and her surviving piglets into the farrowing house and, during the rest of the morning, she produced another fourteen which was taking profligacy to rather vulgar extremes.

I telephoned the oracle and he came rushing across to examine this phenomenon. She was really quite a sight with twenty-two piglets crawling all over her, scrabbling desperately for her fourteen teats. The Guinness Book of Records states that a sow once bore thirty-four young in one litter but twenty-two seemed quite adequate for us. If we could persuade every sow to do that, we could produce twenty-five hundred piglets a year and make our target of £15,000 rather more likely. A thorough investigation in her yard pricked the balloon. There was a skinny sow standing in a corner looking rather bereft, and a quick tug showed that she was in milk. We brought her to join her colleague in the farrowing house and split the mammoth litter between them.

Ted and I almost fell out over these two. He had fixed a basic price for each sow and then added on £4 for every month that they were in pig. Since these sows had farrowed two months earlier than he had calculated, he felt that he should have had some money due to him. I felt that I had some due to me as it was thanks to his incompetence over dates that the sows had given birth in the yard which had resulted in one of the young being squashed. We ended up by calling it quits. I needed Ted's advice too much to push the point and he was getting such tremendous fun out of my balls-ups that he did not want to break our relationship either.

With this second batch of farrowings we had our first home-grown disease problem. The dreaded form of dysentery caused by the *E. coli* family of bugs struck. It only affected one litter but left two of the smaller piglets too weak to stand a chance in the hourly battles for the control of one of their mother's teats. We bought a baby's bottle and started to feed them on a sow's milk substitute. Ted had agreed to look after the farm for a couple of days and this allowed us to take the weekend off to visit relations in Scotland. The two piglets, naturally, came too as they needed four-hourly feeds. They travelled up the motorway curled up round the dog in the back seat of the car and slept most of the way. In Scotland they were installed next to the central heating boiler and created much interest among the local population who came round to view a real live pig. The resident dog brought all its city friends round to have a sniff.

The picture was somewhat marred by one of the piglets having the bad taste to drop dead but there was an untouched hoard of biscuit tins from which to choose a burial casket. The survivor thrived under the warmth and attention that he was given. On our return to the farm, this pig, by now about ten days old and christened Gruntle, was put in solitary splendour in our sick pen with a creep light all to himself. He rapidly became a very expensive little animal. Not being on mother's milk, he grew at an imperceptible rate and showed no interest at all when we tried to introduce him to foster mothers. He would jump out of the creep and stand bellowing by the farrowing house door until he was returned to his own pen.

The only time that he showed any interest in a teat other than that on his bottle was when the dog jumped into his pen to supervise a feed. Gruntle, his greedy little brain probably associating the dog with the comforts of the trip up to Scotland, went rushing up to the dog and sank his teeth into the nearest approximation of a teat that he could find. The dog, a mongrel with a large dash of setter in him, suddenly lost his expression of rather dim arrogance and took off almost vertically with Gruntle hanging on grimly. We put a consoling strip of Elastoplast on the dog but he showed no interest in the opposite sex for several weeks.

By the time that his litter mates were being sold at 60lb, Gruntle was scaling in at a fighting 15lb. We had become tired of his constant demands for attention and gave him the run of the farm, only putting him back in his pen at night. He used to split his time between mocking the slavering sows as they waited for food at the gates in the yard and standing at the back door, beating up the cats and squealing for my wife to bring him his bottle.

When he eventually reached disposable weight, nobody wanted him. He was short, fat and hairy, looking more like an oversized gooseberry than a pig. We thought of putting him in our own deepfreeze but it would have been too much like a cross between infanticide and cannibalism. He would probably have tasted like chewing gum. We sold Gruntle to a back-to-the-land, alternative living, UFO-spotting transcendental meditator and, I was later told, the brutal reality of animal innocence as manifested by Gruntle drove his owner back to Esher and accountancy. Working out the costs of Gruntle was something that I never dared do. The electricity bill alone for two months of continually burning creep bulb would have wiped out any profit that we could have made on him.

Gruntle's headquarters was the sickroom, a small brick-built enclosure which had been constructed to contain coal inside an implement shed. The sickroom was the last view on earth for more than one piglet. Any small animal that showed signs of being off-colour was first placed on top of the stove in the kitchen to warm up and then transported there where it had the choice of either death or recovery. We had another Gruntle-type piglet who became, eventually, quite a respectable animal. He lived in the sickroom for about a month. During the month we were suffering from some kind of fatal epidemic. I would bring in a sickly pig, which would be greeted with delight by the Gruntle-type pig as a potential playmate. The next morning his new companion would be dead and I would have to remove the corpse. After Friend Number Seven the little piglet was beginning to look distinctly hunted and must have thought that he was suffering from a highly pernicious form of B.O.

For about eighteen months after the departure of Gruntle, the boss of the sickroom was a hen. She, along with five companions, was bought from a battery. Initially they would scurry round the yard in a tight feather-to-feather rugby scrum with their heads well down to prevent bashing themselves on the roof of their non-existent cage. Over a couple of weeks it gradually dawned on them that their cage no longer forced them together and they made brave forays by themselves. They were just becoming used to this heady freedom when five of them were polished off by a fox, which must prove something.

The survivor came to the conclusion that a life of freedom was too dangerous and she retreated to the sickroom where she ruled with a beak of iron from the most comfortable corner of the pen.

The pigs, if they were not already dying on arrival, would decide to take an exploratory chew at the hen and receive a beak halfway up their noses in retaliation. If any fighting started up she would wade in and put a stop to it, leaving the protagonists cowering in opposite corners. The only time she left the pen was to lay her daily egg. This she did against the door of the shed so that it would be broken when the door was opened. Latterly, she fed them to the pigs.

Most of the inhabitants of the sickroom came from the weaner pool. It took eighteen months before this was properly organised. Initially, store pigs were kept in some of the little box sheds that were scattered round the yard but, for some very good reason that I cannot remember, we decided to centralise. Our first load of straw was dumped by the haulier in the middle of the yard during a thunderstorm when we were out. From there, I heaved it into the building that had once housed the farm midden in those affluent days when middens had both walls and a roof. This building became the weaner pool; straw bales were put round the walls for extra comfort, and a very attractive looking straw kennel was built at the back. The first batch of piglets behaved at first rather like a bunch of school boys in St Paul's Cathedral, but they soon settled down to some comfortable dunging.

This pen had its little drawbacks. It had a large single-span tin roof which would drop an inch or two with a cracking sound every time a sparrow landed on the ridge. As with most of our buildings, the dung and urine flowed towards the centre rather than the exit, and formed a six-inch-deep pool in which the piglets splashed around on hot, sunny days. The main aggravation came about when we wanted to winkle out those pigs that were ready to be sold.

Chasing unwilling pigs round and round the weaner pool was no fun. The sly ones would crash their way through the straw bales round the wall and play peek-a-boo and king-of-the-castle with their pursuers. The real rats would dive into the swimming pool. Splashing into this fermenting pond to grab a sodden piglet had a nastiness all of its own. Eventually it became too obviously inefficient, even for me, because of the problems associated with mixing piglets of different ages and sizes and the impossibility of cleaning the pen between batches. So we decided to subdivide it and reconcrete it in an attempt to get the falls right.

In doing this we went to town and decided to insulate the floor using some of Bernie's polystyrene sheets which had fallen off the back of a lorry. It was a notable success apart from one or two minor points. The sheets had a tendency to float to the top of the concrete before it had hardened and the depth of concrete over the insulation varied from a foot to half an inch. We also

61

forgot to block the old drain outlet which was several inches below the new floor level. An enterprising rat took residence and, judging from the piles of chewed polystyrene at the drain entrance, honeycombed the underside of the concrete. This led to a few rather unnerving cave-ins. I built more little walls to split up the floor area into five pens and - an amazing technological innovation - suspended water pipes with string from the roof and laid on running water in each pen. This made disposing of the pigs almost a pleasure and our buyer was a much happier man.

The fattener, Dick, was very tolerant in our early days and rarely let his contempt for my incompetence show. The first batch of pigs that he bought from us were the sixty-seven which had spent most of their lives with Ted. Ted gave me a bit of a turn about a week before we were due to sell them by asking me when they were to be castrated. Castration was something that I had read about in the correspondence course, but nobody had mentioned it since. The course was a little out of date so I had assumed that the practice had fallen into disuse - in the same sort of way that it was no longer *de rigueur* to feed Christians to lions. Not a bit of it. We set the day and Ted turned up with a scalpel and an evil grin.

The pigs to be chopped were well beyond the age of consent and the males and the females were beginning to eye each other with knowing glints in their eyes. Fortunately the odd-job man was present and he had muscles where other people did not even have skin. I managed to upend a couple of these oversized beasts while Ted performed his disgusting surgery but then I had to stagger out of the pen suffering from exhaustion and partial deafness brought on by the squeals. I did not, for once, blame the brutes for making a bit of a fuss. Then the odd-job man took over and stood like a rock with sweat pouring off him, occasionally wielding a nifty blade himself. Castration was my least favourite aspect of pig farming. The only inhabitant of the farm who enjoyed it was the dog. He would sit outside the pens quivering with anticipation, snapping up the dainty morsels as they arched through the open door.

A few days later Dick came to take this bunch, giving them a quizzical look as he examined their operation scars. 'You're not meant to do it with your teeth, lad.' Dick, who was a north countryman bearing a striking resemblance to Dennis Healey, would bounce into the yard in his truck every couple of weeks to remove a load of pigs. He would leave the cab and greet me with a big grin and, 'How many, to the nearest dozen, d'you reckon it is this week?'

Counting pigs was an art form at which I never excelled. 'Fifty-five?' I'd hazard.

'Let's have a look at them, then.' He'd examine the pen.

'They're a bit bloody small, aren't they?'

'Nonsense. They're a superb bunch of pigs. Spot on the 60lb.'

'Hmm. We'll soon find out.' I would drag out the scales and put in a 56lb bag of meal with which to calibrate the machine. This turned out to be highly profitable as, after a year of this system, Dick weighed a batch of these bags and found that they averaged over 60lb. He would make conversation while I tried to drive the piglets towards the desired end of the pen.

'Not a bad bit of building, that wall. New, i'n't it?'

'That's right.'

'Who built it?'

'I did,' I would say modestly.

'You did?' There would be complete incredulity in his voice which always managed to irritate me. I was firmly type-cast in his mind as a bumbling idiot, and when I managed to do anything like repair the dumper or build things fairly successfully he would put it on a par with a chimpanzee writing King Lear. We would start to feed the pigs through the scales. This is where the battle of wits would start and it was good-natured but brutal stuff. My wife or his assistant would be standing by with a pen and a notebook to take down the numbers and weight of the pigs. A few would go through without any problems and then I would have to go up the pen to bring down more animals.

'Forty-eight pound,' Dick would sing out as the needle on the scales fluctuated wildly.

'Get on. It was going to settle at about fifty-five.' The pig, in full squeal, would have scuttled up the tailboard of the lorry. 'Are you going to get it back then?' asked Dick as the pig lost itself amongst its fellows already loaded. 'You've got to be on the ball in this game, lad.'

Amazingly, it was all good-humoured stuff and I gave as good as I got. I usually managed to bring my ultimate weapon into play. A pig would dung on the scales. Oh joy! Dick would look at it with distaste and mutter under his breath, calculating the accumulated weight of that dung over the remainder of the pigs and whether it was worth his while to remove it. I always hid all shovels and brushes when he came. The next pig would make as to dung before it mounted the scales. I would slap a hand over the relevant part of its anatomy until it was safely on board where it would drop its load.

Dick's cracking point usually came after three pigs had done their duty. Then he would retire, grumbling, to his wagon and I would put through a quick couple of pigs before he had time to return with his shovel and clean off the muck. Dick's own speciality was jamming the scales with the toe of his boot. Once the pigs escaped from his lorry while we were drinking coffee and fighting over the addition before settling up in the house. When we emerged, they were all sitting calmly on the ground in a corner of the yard with an upturned drum of rat poison beside them. We retired back to the house and argued about whose responsibility the inevitable deaths were to be. Distressingly, they all survived with no ill effects at all, so I changed my brand of poison.

A Run in with the Pigs!

I suppose the lesson of pig farming that we found most difficult to learn was that of shutting gates firmly. In our first year pigs would escape about once a week on average and always take some time to recapture. They would either turn left at the end of the farm lane and I would chase them round and round the slag heaps, or else turn right and end up in the garden of one of the old dears who lived in the bungalows on the road below. I would have to retrieve them stealthily before the escapees completely demolished her vegetable garden.

The local bobby called on us several times to report a strange pig in the vicinity and enquire whether we were one short. Once there were nine thunderous knocks on the door in the middle of the night which sent me rocketing out of bed. It was the policeman. He had found a stray pig earlier in the day and decided that it must have been mine. His method of teaching people to be more careful with their property was to return it at 4 am when he was on night shift. On that occasion the pig did not belong to me and I was rather annoyed. I did not understand why he was giving me rather odd looks until I returned upstairs and found that I had grabbed the wrong dressing gown and was wearing a skimpy, transparent nylon negligee over nothing at all.

My wife quite often heard burglars in the night and dispatched me to investigate. She could never believe that the amazing variety of night noises that echoed round the farmyard could all come from the pigs. One of the strangest came from the sow yards. In winter, when it was chilly, the sows would pile themselves up into heat-retaining mountains of pig flesh. The one at the bottom would eventually have to move because its limbs had gone to sleep and those disturbed would emit roars that would have sounded more appropriate in the Lion Reserve at Woburn. My wife would never believe that this noise was pigs but she was damned if she would ever get out of her nice warm bed to see what it was for herself.

One night she dug me in the ribs and I actually heard the burglar myself. I grabbed the shotgun and went to investigate. In winter I wore a pyjama jacket. In summer, I discarded it. This was a summer burglar. I forgot to put on my spectacles in the rush and tiptoed outside in my gumboots to find the source of the noise. In the darkness I saw an odd-looking blur in the middle of the yard, so I cocked my gun and stealthily approached it. Just then its headlights came on and outlined me stalking it in nothing but a gun and gumboots. The car started up and drove off at high speed.

By the time that I had returned to the front door the dog had shut it behind me and had locked me out. It took about ten minutes to raise my sleeping wife and, by that time, I was decidedly chilly and the mosquitoes were experimenting in some interesting variations to their normal diet. It turned out to be some of Bernie's friends making a late delivery. They never returned, probably through fear of being shot by a naked lunatic. Bernie did not have to pay for the goods and was suitably grateful. I managed to lock myself out in similar circumstances a couple of times, usually while trying to kick the dog's head in when he was having one of those nights in which he decided to howl at the moon for several hours. Eventually I learned to keep a key in one of the outbuildings for such emergencies.

When they were not escaping, the amount of space that the herd required seemed to keep expanding. Fortunately the one thing that we were never really short of was spare sheds. We found that we needed boar pens, pens for odd sows, pens for odd stores, isolation pens, mealhouses and toolsheds as well as the sow yards and multi-suckling pens. One shed that I looked at with some bafflement was the old abreast milking parlour. It had a complicated tangle of tubular metal set on a raised dais which took up half the available floor space.

I lived with it for several months without being able to think of any use for it before I had one of those quantum leaps of lateral thinking. I could hire someone to come along and cut it out. I chatted up one of the reps who promised to send someone along with an oxyacetylene cutter to remove it.

A neighbouring farmer turned up in the yard with a Land Rover and trailer. One of those elliptical business discussions took place. He sucked in his lips as he surveyed the task.

'Cost a fair bit, this will.'

I didn't like the sound of that. I was hoping that the scrap value would just about pay for his labour and gas. 'Oh I don't think so.' I replied.

'What sort of figure had you in mind?'

'Well, I'm not very experienced at pricing things like this. I hoped you might know what was fair.'

He gave me an irritated look. This was obviously not the way I was supposed to do it but I had already discovered through experiences with Dick that the best way to avoid being screwed was to throw yourself on your opponent's mercy when he felt that he could not take unfair advantage of you. He marched round the parlour, fingering the ironwork.

'How about fifty pounds?'

'Fifty pounds - you must be joking.' I had thought a fiver was ample.

'All right then,' he said, 'Seventy-five.'

I felt myself becoming annoyed. The man was treating me like an idiot.

'Don't waste my time. Do you want to cut the bloody thing out or not? If so, you can give me a sensible price. If not, you can take yourself off again.'

'You're a hard man, sir. I'll give you a hundred pounds and not a penny more.'

'What?''

'You heard me, a hundred pounds. That's my top price. I can't give you any more than that.' It was occasions like that which taught me just how green I was. I had been virtually giving away the old cattle troughs and fence posts that cluttered up the buildings and only then did I realise that they should have been worth good money.

The pigs, once the parlour was out, found this shed to be the farm's equivalent of Claridges. They received endless pleasure in lining up at the edge of the concrete dais and shitting over the edge. It fell eighteen inches further than usual and made a highly satisfactory plop. The real joy of the shed was that it had a door that opened directly into the orchard and those privileged pigs whose good behaviour had earned them a tour of duty in this pen were allowed to rootle over its acre and a half to their hearts' content. They could eat the grass during the summer and scrump for apples and pears in the autumn. One year-round delight was wallowing in the ditch and hunting for frogs and tadpoles when they were in season.

Another of the pens was a bit like the Black Hole of Calcutta, built of stone with a low roof and no windows. Local experts, notably the bread lady, told us that it was impossible to house stock in it as they would all die within a couple of weeks. The experts were not clear exactly why, but it turned out to be one of the most successful and popular postings for the pigs. Once inside they could build up a lovely fug that kept them warm on the coldest of days.

The bread lady who, locally, had the authority of Plumb, Macaulay and Gibbon rolled into one, told us that we had a ghost on the farm. Unfortunately he never honoured us with a visit. A hundred-odd years ago a rather dozy farm hand decided to feed the bull without using the bull pen's feeding passage. The bull neatly winkled out his liver with the tip of one of his horns and another soul went to its Maker. The bread lady waxed lyrical about it.

'Horrible it was. My grandmother's father knew him and said there was blood covering the floor and oozing out from under the door. When he was found he was stiff as a board. Stiff as a board with his guts all over the floor. He was a good bull.' We were given this information as she was hunting amongst her meat pies to find the dog its stale biscuit. She paid the dog protection money in the shape of the biscuit each time she called. The one time we had a disagreement the dog did not receive its biscuit and she was bitten.

The ghostly farm hand was supposed to sit in the pen clanking his buckets or something which must drive him to distraction if he has to keep it up for eternity. We turned his pen into a multi-suckling unit, which may have made the ghost a bit huffy, but the feeding passage made a first-class creep. There were a couple of snags about this pen. It had a beautifully laid floor which any dung or urine turned into a skating rink. It also had a hay rack, made of bull-resistant iron, halfway up the wall. When I went in to muck the pen out I would often slide across the floor and bash my head into the rack. The pigs inside were kicked rather more than most and learnt a line in non-Whitehousian language.

In most of these pens we organised creeps by balancing a hurdle along a line of concrete blocks, with a few gaps left in them to act as pop holes for the piglets. In general, it worked very well, but sometimes we got the odd Houdini sow who was maddened by the proximity of the piglets' food and managed, by means unknown, to squeeze through a pop hole and into the creep. Once inside, she would break the light, eat the food, squash a couple of piglets and prove quite impossible to extricate without dismantling the creep, which took about an hour.

For the first year or so, we found buying tools, equipment and the odd bits and pieces that go into a farm very difficult. A lifetime of warming a chair in an office and commuting is no help at all when it comes to pricing gates, nuts and bolts or straw. Screws had always been things that came in little packets of five priced at 20p and you broke your fingernails trying to get them out. When we needed a hundred screws, I would go out to buy twenty little packets. The discovery that they could be bought in large boxfuls opened up new horizons.

It was the same sort of thing with gates. We had to buy ten of them, mainly to support the walls in the sow yards. One of those shady individuals who sells gates off the back of a truck visited us and we bought them from him. I have since found out that you can always negotiate a discount of at least 50 per cent on these sort of gates and anyway they were totally unsuitable for restraining sows. It did not occur to me that they would rust and they began to fall to bits within a few weeks. The pigs were given a great deal of amusement by these gates. They chewed holes in them, tossed them off their hinges and swung on them. The only way that they were kept remotely secure was by festooning them with barbed wire which meant that I cut my hands every time that I opened them.

My other attempt at pig-proof gates was to invest in some expensive hardwood doors for the weaner pool. These lasted for all of five days until, one morning, I found heads poking through the middle of each of them, demanding to be fed. Sometimes we did not make the same mistake twice and in this case we tacked slabs of cast iron to the interior of each, which gave the inmates days more pleasure before they learned to chew out the supports and break through once more.

One morning, one of these pens contained a dead piglet. It always put me in a bit of a dilemma when that happened. Should I cross fingers and hope that it was just an isolated incident or take it along for a post mortem to discover if it was a victim of some ghastly form of porcine plague that was about to decimate the herd. We had an expert, as usual, on the farm - this one was the scrap man who with a pony and cart chugged round the farms and rubbish tips that filled the gaps between the slag heaps, making a very good living. He decided that a post mortem would be a very good idea and tacked a horseshoe on the door of the farrowing house to help preserve the inmates from the epidemic to come.

We took the pig's remains to the vet and he decided to hold on to it to make some tests. After a bit of shopping we returned to the farm. On our approach we noticed some smoke above the trees. This was not unusual. On roasting days the crematorium smoke would quite often drift over the area and fill the minds of the retired inhabitants of the bungalows with gloomy thoughts about their futures.

This particular column of smoke was rather thicker than usual, even for a Monday. We hurtled up to the farm and found that the entire hundred-foot length of the building that dominated the middle of the yard was in flames. Inside was the farrowing house and three other pens. There was a batch of eleven sows due any moment. In fact two of them had already produced twenty-one piglets. There were a couple of odd porkers at one end, fattening for the Christmas deep-freeze trade and, right in the middle, Gruntle.

We pulled up in the yard, piled out of the car, appalled at the violence of the fire, and ran towards the house and telephone. I barely had time to get through the front door when the first fire engine arrived. It had been called by the stoker of the crematorium, incensed at the sight of a rival funeral pyre. Before the firemen had time to unclip their hoses the slate roof of the barn crashed down into the interior. The barn was about 150 years old and the nice dry woodwork, particularly the wooden boards of the first floor on which we stored our straw, could have been specifically designed to feed the flames.

The most striking aspect of the blaze was the immense volume of sound that it produced. We had to shout to make ourselves heard above the roar and crackle of the flames and the screams of the pigs trapped inside. A mixture of shirt-sleeves and sheer fright prevented me approaching the building too closely. The firemen were better protected, both morally and physically. A couple of them went inside to see if the animals could be pulled out. I borrowed a helmet and jacket and plucked up the courage to follow them in.

The whole area of the farrowing house was bright with flames. They had a frightening beauty as they shimmered across the ceiling and the roof supports. In one corner the falling slates had come through the fire-weakened timbers of the first floor, leaving a gaping hole to the sky through which the flames thundered, using it as a chimney.

The fire had not gained a strong hold at the end of the building where the porkers were living and they were led out without any problem. The sows were a different proposition. They were underneath the raging heart of the fire in their farrowing crates. Of the eleven animals, we managed to get two out with considerable difficulty. We could not persuade them to leave their crates. Terror had sent them chasing up to the front of them and the only way that we could make them back out was by waving bits of burning material in their faces. One of the evacuees collapsed and died as she came out of the barn and the other was led away to await the arrival of the vet. We went back inside just as a further section of the first floor collapsed, sending me skittering out to safety and even causing the firemen to back rather warily outside.

By this time another two fire engines had arrived, connected a web of hoses from the stream and were pouring gallons of water over the flames. One of the dangers was that the fire might jump the ten-foot gap between the gable end of the barn and the house. I suddenly remembered Gruntle. He was, at the time, in a little pen just off the farrowing house. I put my hard hat back on and went in to look for him. For added protection one of the firemen gave me a split-second blast of the hose that nearly blew me right through the barn and out the other side. Gruntle's pen was a couple of feet deep in fallen slates, burning straw and rafters. I called rather hopelessly for him and out of the shambles he paddled, yelling for his bottle. The slates had fallen in such a way that they had formed a well-protected cubic foot of cubbyhole which, with his luck, was just where he was standing when the roof fell in.

I suppose it must have taken the fire brigade about half an hour to control the blaze sufficiently to allow us to re-enter the building without the danger of being squashed by burning beams coming down from the roof. There was very little left. The interior of the building had been gutted with a network of charred timbers between the floor and the sky. The farrowing crates were still there with their occupants inside them. One slight consolation, according to the firemen, was that the animals would have been asphyxiated before the heat had reached them. The one survivor had been under a lean-to section of the roof and so had missed the collapse of the roof as well as receiving oxygen and a speedy rescue through the nearby door. The twenty-one piglets had vanished without trace.

It was then that a touch of badly needed comedy entered the arena to help lift the depression. This came from the police. The first on the scene was a uniformed constable contained in a panda car. He looked at the scene with alarm and summoned help in the shape of a CID inspector and his straight man. They suspected arson. I was in a rather awkward position. For a start, I had recently come to the attention of the local police in the form of a sheaf of unpaid parking tickets which had finally caught up with me from London. I had also been caught red-handed in not renewing my car licence in time. The police had not very far to go to uncover their number one suspect.

An interested group of locals had gathered to watch the excitement and the police filtered amongst them as unobtrusively as elephants to look for a twitching fire bug. Nobody came leaping out of the crowd shouting 'Look no further, it was I,' and so they retired to their incident room which they set up in my office and summoned me for questioning. With much licking of pencils, the constable took my statement while the inspector listened in the background. I was in a bit of a hurry as there was plenty that I should have been doing in the yard but the Law was not to be rushed. He set me down, adjusted the desk light so that it shone in my eyes and carefully read my statement. The sergeant came in and whispered something in his ear. Then my interrogation began.

'You came here from London, I believe?'

'That's right.'

'Are your buildings insured?'

'Yes.' This was what added to the awkward position in which I found myself.

'When did you get them insured?'

'About a fortnight ago.'

He looked severely at me. 'Why did you get them insured?'

'So that I would get some money if they caught fire.'

'Quite a coincidence that they went up so soon after.'

'Yes.' I had to agree with him. His next question took me by surprise but I swear he really asked it.

'Do you know anyone called Kray?'

'What?'

'Do you know anyone called Kray? It's a simple question. I want to know if you were involved with any of the London gangs.'

'Certainly not.'

'Pity. I was wondering if they might want revenge on you for some reason.'

'No, I'm sorry. I can't think of anyone who might want to burn me out.'

He switched tactics. 'Did you start the fire yourself?'

'No.' I was too sharp to be caught out that way.

'Have you got any petrol lying about the place?'

'No.'

His head snapped up. 'Sergeant!' he called. The sergeant came forward carrying a gallon of petrol. 'We found this in a cupboard in the next-door building. Is it yours?'

'Yes.'

'Ha,' he said triumphantly. 'Why were you lying just now?'

'I'd forgotten about that. We use it for the motor mower, rather than for burning down barns.' 'Burning down barns,' he wrote in his notebook. 'But,' I went on, 'if I did use that petrol to set the barn off, I would most likely use it all and not leave the tin half-full.'

Quick as a flash, he came back. 'How did you know that the tin was still half-full?'

'It is my tin, so I ought to know.'

This conversation went on for half an hour before my interrogator decided that I was too tough a nut for him to crack. He excused me and returned to the yard to find more suspects. Ted was hauled in as a highly suspicious character when he was poking round the ruins to see if he could do anything to help. I sprung him after ten minutes. They then found a Jehovah's Witness who had the misfortune to be canvassing for souls down at the bungalows. The Witness had a witness and he escaped quite easily.

The next prime suspect was Bernie. He appeared after a morning in the pub, well brewed up. The police fell on him with cries of delight. 'Bernie, you horrible little villain, you dropped your lighter.' Poor Bernie, he had an extremely uncomfortable half-hour until I managed to dig up a couple of people who had been in the bar with him during the crucial period and were able to give him an alibi.

Eventually, in a final attempt to trap me a day or two after the fire, the police trundled out a gleaming bemedalled chief superintendent. I could not help thinking that this dazzling figure might have better things to do than visit seedy pig farmers. Anyway he came with his bristly white moustache and paced up and down beside the remains of the building slapping his thigh with a pair of leather gloves, firing penetrating questions at me in a brisk I-brook-no-nonsense tone. His first question - again I swear he really asked it - was 'Do you smoke?' I took the pipe out of my mouth and answered in the affirmative. He went on for ten minutes or so with a semi-circle of admiring underlings around him before he placed a boot in a pile of pigshit, whereupon he lost interest.

Once the blaze was out, the firemen damped down the wreckage and posed proudly for the photographer from the local paper. Bernie fell off a fire engine and broke his arm. The departing police took him to hospital. The knacker went through the grisly business of winching the dead sows on to his wagon. The vet came and ministered to the surviving sow and, eventually, they all departed. At about 7 pm one of the firemen returned with half a dozen elderly gentlemen. They were all retired firemen who had come to view the remains and they dicussed animatedly over the cups of coffee that we provided for them how much better the fire would have been handled in their day and how all the excitement and romance had gone out of the business.

During the night following the fire we were kept awake by the sound of falling timbers and bricks. The next morning the vet revisited the sow. She was in a pretty bad way. She was flat out and her breathing was laboured with a bloody froth at her nostrils. The vet put this down to lung damage caused by inhaling the superheated air, for which there was not a great deal he could do. Over the next few days, the skin on one side gradually sloughed off and she ate and drank nothing. Amazingly, she survived and produced five healthy piglets a week later. She went on to become one of the most prolific and best-natured animals on the farm.

The next action we took was to contact the insurance company. We were told to leave everything as it was until the adjusters had been to see us. It was not very cheering stuff. The barn dominated the farmyard. It was impossible to get the smell of it out of your nostrils. We had two depressing days before the expert turned up. The cause of the fire was still not clear but he put it down to an electrical fault caused by the wiring which had just been renewed. Clearly food for thought and litigation. He was followed by an electrical expert, a dear old man who was half-blind and needed me to point out where the fire might have started. After a bit of prompting, the expert departed convinced that the local Electricity Board who had installed our new creep lights were at fault.

The board had by this time got wind of what was afoot and a posse of their own experts descended but, surprise surprise, they decided that their wiring was not to blame. The two sets of adjusters then had to arrive at an agreed figure so that they would know how much they had to sue each other for. It was pretty depressing from our point of view. The value at risk was put at £28,000 and I had insured for only £5,000, which is probably why I am not in jail. They reckoned that the barn was three-quarters destroyed - the shell was still standing. The insurance company paid what they thought they owed me and the value of the stock lost. I was to receive the balance after they had sued the Electricity Board for the full amount.

The incentive was certainly there for us but, after eighteen months of bickering, my insurance company eventually decided that their case against the board would not stand up in court. The cause was never really established. Some of the board experts tried to blame it on a bursting creep light but there were only two alight at the time and neither were near the seat of the fire. Another theory that they mooted was that one of the creep lights had a totally unsuitable flex that had caused the fire. I had bought the installation off Ted and we allowed them to commit themselves deeply to this theory before producing evidence which proved that they themselves had installed the flex on Ted's farm.

After the shouting had died away we had a conference to decide on our next move. We had lost the farrowing house and three other sheds and were to receive about £3,500 back. There were a few possibilities. We could attempt to rebuild but that would cost a great deal more money than we had available. We could partially rebuild. The idea there was that we would pull the building down to the first-floor level and put a flat roof over it. Initially we went ahead with this one.

For a really satisfying job, there can be little to beat demolition work. With Bernie's help - he was damned if he was going to miss out on the fun even with one arm in plaster - I slung a rope round the gable, tied the other end to the dumper and pulled. Absolutely nothing happened first time and so I took a run at it. This time the rope snapped taut, bringing the dumper to a sudden halt and lifting its back wheels off the ground. I sailed over the steering wheel and landed in the skip which had, as always, an inch-thick coating of putrefying dung covering its surface. After a bath, I returned to the fray and eventually the entire gable tottered over and crashed to the ground. It was glorious fun.

Bernie then found three brand-new sledgehammers lying abandoned in a ditch and with these we moved steadily along the top of the wall knocking out bricks. One visitor got a bit carried away with the feeling of power and knocked out below first-floor level and was made to build it back up again which was not nearly such joy. While this was going on we salvaged the farrowing crates from the interior, repainted them and put in new floors.

Before we started to rebuild we had an expert in to make sure that there would be no problems. He told us that the mortar had been severely weakened throughout the structure and would have to be replaced before we could put any weight on the walls. At this, we gave up and decided to demolish the building entirely. I was not really sorry as the truncated barn would always have been a reminder of the fire and it would have taken months to be rid of the smell. In addition, its removal would leave us with a much more open yard and relieve the feeling that we were living in the middle of a claustrophobic shanty town of sheds of all shapes and sizes. It would also leave us with a much better view of the slag heaps.

We obtained quotations for its disposal from half a dozen contractors. The top price was £950 - the bottom £170. After not too much thought we accepted the lower price. The only condition was that it would be up to me to find a site on which to dump the rubble.

The contractor turned up at 8 am on a Saturday with two caterpillar vehicles and a couple of lorries. In no time there was rising above the wreck site a cloud of dust which almost rivalled the original smoke. We had neighbours darting about pinching bricks and slates as they presented themselves. Farmers were efficient recyclers of waste for years before the environmentalists thought of the idea and many local farms were embellished by bits of the barn. In addition, it was the father of half a pub extension, a garage roof and a pigeon loft.

We ran into a problem when we were banned from the local rubbish tips. Slag and used drums of cyanide were perfectly alright but the contractor knew what he had been about when he left the dump site up to me. I had to scurry round the locality to find a new spot. This was during the middle of a building strike and there was a bypass being built round the nearby town. Its untenanted stretches provided an ideal site.

The first lorry driver to dump his load there became stuck and his equally bright mate bogged down in the mud when he tried to pull him out. I, being the only person present without a clue, was called in to supervise the extraction. We saw an abandoned JCB about a mile further down the road, and trudged through the mud of the unpaved road suface to borrow it when nobody was looking. When we arrived, we discovered that neither I nor the two lorry drivers had any idea how to work the thing so we trudged all the way back to the farm and used one of the contractor's machines. It took only half a day to get going once more.

We then found a rather more suitable stretch of bypass with a more solid surface; we crossed the site attendant's palm with silver so that he would deny ever seeing us and started dumping again. This stretch was already graded ready for the tarmac but, by the time that we had finished, there were forty truckloads of rubble plopped along it at neat intervals rather like the droppings from a gargantuan hen. I would have loved to have seen the faces of the construction crews after they returned to work with their mammoth rise. We used to think fondly of the departed when we travelled over the new road. Four miles of motorway was not a bad tombstone.

The demolishers were very quick but the job was not without its hazards. From one of the bulldozers a wire hawser with a great metal hook on its end was slung round a piece of building to pull it down: the sort of thing that I had tried to do with the dumper except on a much larger scale. The hawser snapped just above the hook and was catapulted across the yard, straight through a shed, between two startled pigs and out through the closed door on the opposite side.

It took three days to remove all traces of the barn and it left us with a large prairie in the middle of the yard. As Ted said, you felt like taking a packed lunch every time you set out to cross it.

We pinched some topsoil from the edge of the stream and dumped it in the hole with some grass seed and a sapling in the middle. It was as if the barn had never been. I even found the horseshoe that the scrap man had carefully nailed to the door of the barn on the morning of the fire. I carefully affixed it to the stake of the sapling for more good luck.

The greatest beneficiaries of the fire were the pigs that had not been directly involved. They had about three weeks of viewing some splendid goings on. After their breakfast they would all line up at the pen gates and spend the day observing our antics. It is not only the human race which is diverted by construction and demolition. Their only regret must have been that we were unable to provide a finale that could equal the overture.

The firemen had a ball. The police had fun emulating Inspector Clouseau. The adjusters and the Electricity Board got themselves work which they were able to spin out for eighteen months. Even I felt rich putting a fat insurance cheque into the bank and receiving a congratulatory letter from my bank manager. The only losers were the pigs who were inside the building when it went up. If it had not been for them we might have tried repeating the exercise every few months.

The 'Boar' Wars

With the fire behind us we had to return to the serious business of making a living from the pigs. Where to create a new farrowing house was not hard to decide. The sows were turfed out of the old cubicle shed and the farmer who had bought the milking parlour turned up with his chequebook to remove the metal partitions. Losing all the sows that were due to farrow at least gave us a month's breathing space to prepare the quarters before the next batch was due. We cemented in the crates, built little walls between the creeps out of salvaged bricks and put down lots of concrete to try to make most of the piddle go in the right direction. We even invited the Electricity Board to install the new creep lights and this time we had testers and inspectors coming and going for weeks.

One of the irritations arising from the fire was that all the electricity had been channelled through the burnt barn and this meant that almost every building on the place had to be rewired. Another irritation rapidly turned out to be the new lawn in the centre of the yard. When we came to fill in the hole left by the barn the midden had been rather full and so we shifted it in its entirety to provide a foundation. This was a mistake. The muck rapidly rotted and a stroller needed crampons and climbing boots to walk across the lawn. We also had the fastest growing grass in the United Kingdom and hired a brace of tethered rabbits to keep it under some sort of control.

With our new sophistication produced by experience, we even went as far as insulating our new farrowing house. Bernie's contacts produced another load of free polystyrene and we tacked it up over all the walls and roof. The sows and mice loved it. The pigs tore it down in great chunks and ate it while the mice organised conventions and sex orgies between the roof and the insulation. Stalking the noise with a sharp-pointed dung-fork at the ready to stab through the polystyrene became a favourite and absorbing bloodsport, particularly for guests.

Somewhat to my surprise, the pigs turned out to be very definite individual characters. The boars shone out above the others mainly, I suppose, because I was so terrified of them at the beginning that I kept a very close eye on them. We had seven boars at various times. There was a Saddleback which we disposed of fairly early on. George, Fred, Ben, Alf and Ron were Large Whites and Duke was a Landrace. The Granddaddy was Bert. When we bought him, he was about seven years old which was quite an age for a pig.

Apparently he had distinguished himself at the outset of his career by leaping off the lorry which had brought him to Ted's farm and rogering four separate sows one after the other until he had collapsed through sexual exhaustion. When we bought him he had slowed down a bit but he was still utterly dependable provided he was not rushed. Bert's great quality was his complete reliability. In his old age he had become weary of the wiles of the fairer sex and did not waste his time with foreplay. When I asked him to perform his duty he would come out of his pen and jump straight onto the back of the indicated sow and get on with the job. If I was standing around in the snow or the driving rain Bert's speed was very much appreciated.

I found the mating habits of the pig really rather remarkable. The oddest part of it was the shape of the boar's equipment. If there is any other animal that has a corkscrew stuck on the sharp end, I have yet to come across it. Another peculiarity was the length of time that it took a boar to complete the service. I had seen the odd bull carrying out its duty, and if you blinked your eye at the wrong moment the only way that you could tell that the deed had been done was the air of smugness on the face of both the bull and the cow.

The boar jumped on the sow readily enough but then appeared to go to sleep for about twenty minutes before a gentle shiver announced the crucial moment. The pig farmer is supposed to stand around and keep an eye on things, making sure that the boar does not go up the wrong passage or commit various other elementary blunders. I bought a pair of plastic gloves for use in such situations but the boredom of watching the boar doing his stuff was akin to watching an extremely bad blue film being run at quarter speed with Swedish subtitles.

Fred, boar, son of Bert, had an altogether nastier disposition. He was the only boar that ever really got cross with me and tried to sort me out. More than once he forced me to float over a wall like Nureyev to avoid losing the seat of my pants. The boars' duty was to serve the sows but they first had to check whether any of them were on heat. Fred used to become exceedingly annoyed if none of the sows were on heat after I had summoned him from his after breakfast nap.

We arranged our system of service round the feeders, releasing the sows that we thought might be on heat one by one, and putting the boars to them until they had been served twice as the regulations demanded. The method was almost faultless. If more than one sow was on heat, those still locked up in the feeders would become a bit randy at the sight of another having it away and start roaring and frothing with frustration. Occasionally the boar would be feeling particularly frisky and attempt to serve the same sow twice or even have a go at anything that moved including me, but generally it worked without a hitch.

Fred was the only boar who could make the system dangerous. I could always tell when Fred was feeling particularly randy because he would start to hop around on three legs. Whenever I saw that happen I had to find a fruity sow double quick or be prepared to take the consequences. If the selected sow should prove not to be on heat this archetypal male chauvinist pig would start to beat her up. When I moved in to separate them he would relieve his frustration by chasing me round the yard. To give Fred his due, he was ruled entirely by his libido which is all that can be really asked of a boar.

George, on the other hand, reckoned that sex came a very poor second to the delights of food. He was the boar that arrived on the farm with the first batch of sows and fell in love with

Number Eleven to the exclusion of all else. He was not even particularly good at his job. George was fickle. One day he would be demanding his sow and the next, when there were sows begging for his attentions, he would refuse to do the gentlemanly thing. He really was astonishingly greedy and the pangs of hunger led him to become the farm's most accomplished escapologist. If you waved a scoopful of meal within a hundred yards of him he would bash down doors and trample sows underfoot in his eagerness to get to you.

Three or four times he escaped from pens that appeared to be totally secure and was found in the mealshed. No door has yet been built that could stand the assault of half a ton of pig flesh ramming it at a good 25mph and George would be found insensible with the door in splinters and a gut on him like a balloon, having consumed half a hundredweight of meal. After his blowouts I would drag him back to his pen behind the dumper and he would remain there gasping for a couple of days before being back on his feet squealing for food again. The privilege of being allowed to use the orchard was forbidden to him. He only used it as a more convenient place from which to escape to the mealhouse, usually dragging several yards of fence with him.

Nothing came before George's stomach. The only way that I could superintend his services was by knocking a hole in the brick wall that surrounded the sow yards and peering through. If he caught sight of me he would jump off the sow's back and come trotting over, squealing for food. The sows found this behaviour quite outrageous and would chase after him, roaring and biting. George surprised us all by dying in the night. The post mortem report stated that it was due to an acute stomach upset, which was not unexpected.

Alf was the first boar that we bought ourselves and proved to be the friendliest pig that we ever owned. He was a mere baby of six months old when we took delivery of him and he still considered the sows to be potential mothers rather than sex objects. Even when his balls did drop he hadn't a clue. The experts gave all sorts of helpful suggestions about how to teach a boar to do what should have come naturally, like giving him a grandstand view of Bert in action, or penning him up with some raddled old hag with plenty of experience to bust his cherry for him. The only piece of advice we did not take was to turn him out with an older boar so that he could pick up hints. In our experience, that would be just a quick way to end up with a dead pig.

We tried all the tricks we knew but the technique totally eluded him, although he could not be faulted for enthusiasm. His most shaming moment came when, in full view of the rest of the pigs, we put him out with the herd nymphomaniac at her fruitiest. Alf trotted round her, squealing with excitement at the delicious perfumes she was emitting, while she stood like a statue waiting for him to mount her. Eventually the sow went down on her front knees - an action which I had never seen before and have never seen since - and waved her vagina at him like a bullseye. Alf still did not catch on and we had to lead him away amid the raucous derision of his peers.

Alf eventually decided that sexual satisfaction was in some way connected with leaning against the head of the sow and one day, when he was enjoying a particularly titillating lean, I risked a rupture by bodily lifting him into position Number One of the porcine Kama Sutra and holding him there until nature took over. From then on he was a raging sex machine.

Alf's offspring were of noticeably higher quality than what we had been used to and we were delighted with him. Alf had certain little games which he liked to play. When not on top of a sow, happiness was trotting round the yard with a visitor on his back. He would never tire of this and would squeal furiously if the visitor got off. The rider would then hurriedly remount to prevent himself being torn to bits. His other favourite hobby was teasing the dog who used to mooch around the sow yards and fall asleep just outside the pen gates. Alf would tiptoe up and grab the dog's tail which gave him enormous pleasure and the dog none at all. The dog never learned to stay away and this could happen a couple of times a day.

Alf grew up to be a huge animal with a strong sense of his own importance and hated to lose face in front of his ladies. He also had a yellow streak a mile wide. Once he was in a pen with seven or eight sows and he managed to break out when another pen of pigs was in the feeders. I saw him come trotting up the passage towards the food and yelled 'Alf' in tones of fury. He came skidding to a halt and ran back to his pen squeaking in terror. When I arrived at the pen gate to resecure it, he was trotting round the sows roaring at them which, in pig language, means, 'I am enormously virile and am in complete control of the situation.' He can only have been afraid that his harem had witnessed his craven exhibition and was explaining how they had misunderstood his behaviour.

On another occasion Alf decided to break out of his pen at about 6 am - well before we had woken up. We heard grunts on the stairs and there was Alf halfway up on his way to our bedroom. Friendliness and having a meaningful relationship with the pigs was all very well, but we had to draw a line somewhere. Sharing a bedroom with a boar was some way beyond it. He had knocked the catch on the door and although the opportunity for mayhem was considerable, he had left not a trace of mess or damage downstairs apart from scoffing a loaf of bread in the kitchen. He even appeared to have wiped his feet before coming in as the carpets were spotless.

The two other boars, Ron and the Saddleback, never really shone as individuals. The Saddleback looked too like his sows and we did not keep him long enough to get to know him. Ron was a rather simple soul, full of good intentions but rather dull with it. He walked with a waddle which looked rather peculiar but never interfered with his effectiveness.

The last boar that we bought was the Landrace, Duke, and he turned out to be a real star. He was bigger than any other pig on the farm and made even Alf look like a mere porker. Before we acquired him he had already performed long and faithful service for another breeder. He had bought Duke to serve his Saddle-back sows, producing crossbred gilts which were to supersede the purebred Saddlebacks. This meant that their progeny would be white rather than 'blue' and would make a longer and leaner carcass. The only reason that we were able to buy him was that he had run out of wives and would have had to start serving his own daughters, a consummation within the prohibited degrees of kindred and affinity even in pigs.

We looked at his offspring and bought him without hesitation. His daughters' beauty was the more surprising when you looked at him. He was no oil painting. Apart from his bulk, he had a hunchback, brought on, I was told because he had spent so much of his life bent over the back of sows. He had great folds in his skin like a rhinoceros. He paddled around on feet like dinner plates. Rather like a horse, a pig is supposed to have a nice straight leg and a mincing foot. In Duke's case, the hocks, pasterns or whatever his ankles should have been called, had gone, which was usually a pig's ticket to the abattoir, but it did not seem to bother him in the slightest.

We put him in one of the three cottage sties at the back of the house we used as isolation pens in case any new arrival was carrying any nasty diseases. He soon proved himself a pig of immense gentility. If he was visited, he would come out of his kennel to have his ear scratched. He cocked his head on one side to have a good look from under his lop ears before allowing himself to be tickled. This could be rather disconcerting as one of his eyes was blue and the other brown.

When he was fed in the morning he would courteously wait until all the meal had been emptied from the bucket into the trough before he would eat. Every other pig that we owned came snorting out at the first sniff of food and would have ended up with most of it on its head. Duke only blew it once. Ted took over the farm one weekend when we went away. He sent his wife out to feed the pigs while he stayed in bed. He always was a bright lad. His wife went into the sty to feed Duke and he must

87

have recognised an unknown quantity.

He came galloping out of his kennel, knocked her flat on her back and stood over her with his front legs on either side of her neck. She closed her eyes and composed herself ready to meet her Maker, while Duke carefully sniffed her chin and gave her a smacking kiss. This was too much and she slapped his face. Duke gave a deep disappointed sigh and moved back. She scrambled to her feet and went to bed for the rest of the day to recover from the shock. Ted, much to his disgust, had to feed the rest of the herd.

We had two complaints about Duke. He did like making love in bed. Each of the sow yards had a kennel at the back where I had built a couple of walls about four or five feet high roofed over with straw bales. The sows would retire into them at night and build up a nice fug. When Duke felt randy in the middle of the night he would jump on the back of his nearest bed partner and erupt through the roof, bringing the bales cascading down. The roars of annoyance from the rest of the sows echoed round the farmyard and woke the neighbours half a mile away.

He was also rather cavalier in his treatment of his wives. Duke's idea of being sexy was to come galumphing up to a sow and take a jump at her. The result of the best part of a ton of pigmeat landing on the back of the unfortunate sow can be imagined and Duke squashed several promising romances before we put him on a strict diet. He must have lost 100lb which helped a bit, but I still had to interpose my body, in the best Strachey tradition, between him and his beloved to blunt the impetus of his initial charge. I then had to try to persuade him to step more decorously into position.

Quite early on we discovered that boars did not mix. This became evident during service when the boars that were not actually performing would stand by the gates of their pens, gnashing their teeth and foaming at the lucky one who was actually having it away. The first boar meet was when Fred encountered the Saddleback. I had released a pen of sows and had forgotten that the boar was amongst them. Fred came trotting past the Saddleback boar and as he caught a whiff of his business end he did a double take and came skidding to a halt. Fortunately I had noticed my error and was right behind him with the dung-fork and gave him the bum's rush back to his pen before he had time to collect his wits for the punch-up.

The next encounter was a bit messier. Fred was by himself in a pen adjacent to Bert and a batch of sows. Bert was supposed to be checking them in case any of them had come back onto heat showing that their initial brace of servings had not taken. During the night Fred's libido went out of control and he ploughed his way through the nine-inch block wall between the pens. When I arrived in the morning at feeding time the place looked like a ketchup factory. There had been a titanic battle between the boars and Bert had been the loser. All the sows were cowering in a corner while Fred was pacing round their pen roaring. He had half an ear missing and was pouring blood from several gashes in his body.

Bert had gone back through the hole that Fred had made in the wall and was sitting in the corner rather like a dog, shivering with his head facing the wall. He had obviously put up a good fight to defend his honour and that of his sows but his old bones had just not been up to a fight with his son. Bert was pathetically glad to see me and started grunting softly with a fearful eye on the hole in the wall to make sure he did not antagonise the victorious Fred who was strutting up and down guarding the gap.

I opened the pen door and helped the poor old beast to his feet and he limped across the yard to an empty store pen. We piled it full of straw and left him to recover. By afternoon he had stiffened up completely and was flat out on his side unable to move. He lay like that for three days before he started to improve. During that time he was completely helpless and we had to feed him by hand. We would prop his great head on a lap and gently spoon meal down his throat and chase it down with the hose pipe, full on.

89

The sad part about the episode was Bert's loss of confidence in his boarhood. He was back on his feet within a week, but it took him two more to summon up the courage to serve a sow. What set him up again was an encounter through a gate with Fred. Bert woofed and Fred retreated. He did his first sow straight afterwards but the old speed and fluency of technique never came back. One point that made me feel rather smug was that the collapsed wall had been built by the perfectionist odd-job man. I rebuilt it and put iron rods inside the concrete blocks set down into the ground. It would have taken a tank to shift it after that.

The second boar fight took place between Fred and George. Fred was having a pleasant amorous interlude when George must have thought that he had heard the chink of the meal scoop and came charging out. I was alerted by the racket and a terrified electrician who was wiring up the new farrowing house. The two boars were rolling all over the yard trying to tear chunks out of each other. There was an eighteen-foot hurdle fairly handy; the electrician took hold of one end, I grabbed the middle and we charged them. The impact knocked them apart with the hurdle between them. George seemed to be quite glad of the interruption and sat tight trying not to look belligerent in case Fred vaulted over to attack him once more. Fred was furious at the interference. After all, he had not started the fight. He came trotting down the hurdle to sort us out. We dropped it and bolted. The electrician ran into a pen with the foaming Fred at his heels and jumped over the wall at the far end. While Fred was engaged in trying to scale the wall after him, I slammed and bolted the door and left him to cool off. A quick rattle of cake cubes and George was safely in the pen next door.

The final boar fight was something of a fiasco. At the time George was living in the bull pen which had an iron bar across the door to keep it shut. He would spend most of the day standing on his back legs and leaning on the door so that he could keep a close eye on the mealhouse which was on the other side of the yard. We had sold Bert to another farmer and he was going to spend his retirement in charge of a group of six sows.

We were leading him past George's pen towards his new owner's vehicle and trailer when George's head popped up above the door and he started to make rude noises at Bert. Bert got cross, trotted over and flipped the bar off the door which brought George tumbling out into the yard, and Bert got in a swift chop. Bert's new owner had taken to his heels. George thought that this was not a bad idea and followed him. Bert followed George roaring, and I followed Bert with a broom.

The farmer thought that George was after him. George knew that Bert was chasing him, and so we did a couple of circuits of the yard at high speed. Bert and I became a bit puffed and we both dropped out for a bit of a rest while George and the farmer continued. George then caught a whiff of the mealhouse which took him out, leaving the farmer alone in the race. He made for the cab of his Land Rover and refused to emerge until George was rounded up and Bert was safely locked into the trailer.

I often thought that a good deal of money could be made from organising boar fights. It would be akin to fighting cocks except a lot more spectacular. We were fairly lucky with our boars and never had a really cantankerous specimen. One of my neighbours was cornered by one of his boars in a feeding passage. In his hands he had an old pitchfork, the prongs of which had worn and become exceedingly sharp. When the boar moved towards him chomping its jaws he prodded it in the face. The boar did not even blink but kept on coming. He really drove the fork in and the animal wrenched it from his hands and charged him. A pigman heard the racket and threw a sack over the boar's head. The farmer survived, only needing twenty stitches. If I had known beforehand that boars did that sort of thing, I would never have gone pig farming.

Pig Parenting

The sows, on the whole, were never quite such interesting characters as the boars. They had a very strict hierarchy amongst themselves and right at the top of the ladder was Number Seven. She was a massive pig who bullied the rest of the sows unmercifully and was the only one that ever maliciously bit me. I had been warned of the dangers of boars and was always careful with them but my initial fear of the sows wore off after a couple of months of peaceful coexistence. It was, therefore, a considerable surprise when Number Seven came out of the kennel when I was performing my principal agricultural duty of being the herd lavatory attendant and inflicted a gash on my leg.

That was one of the dangers if your relationship with farm stock became too casual. They would cease to regard you as human and the boss and treat you as another member of the herd who ought to be kept in his place. It was sheer bloodymindedness on her part and, in the same sort of way you are supposed to remount a horse after falling off, I went straight back into her pen with blood pouring down my leg and beat the living daylights out of her with a chunk of wood when she came at me again.

Number Seven produced quite good litters, but her size was such that she could hardly fit inside the farrowing crate. I put her on diet after diet but she must have had some sort of hormonal or glandular imbalance because she just kept on growing fatter. Her end came when she farrowed and produced one miserable little pig and we disposed of her.

The other sow that bit me was 159. Actually knowing which sow was which could be rather difficult. They were all black with a white band round their middles. It took a few months before we could differentiate one from the other without a careful examination. In theory there should have been no problem since each animal had a large plastic tag in its ear. In practice the tags would fall out, get chewed by their next-door neighbour or become covered in dung. 159 turned out to be 28 with a dirty black mark on her tag being the hundred. By the time that we discovered she had been using an alias she was inextricably 159 and so she remained.

She was a really charming pig and always appeared delighted to see me. That is a trait that totally disarms me when I come across it in domestic animals. As a farmer, my purpose was to exploit the animals as far as possible and I could not afford to become emotionally involved in them. But when a pig starts to follow you round like a lap dog and rolls over on its back to have its stomach scratched, it can be very difficult to remain detached. 159 bit me when I was putting in some fresh straw and I brushed against her. She obviously thought I was another pig and as she was quite high up in the pecking order she took a quick automatic snap at my boot. When she realised it was me and not another sow, she was quite overcome with embarrassment and remorse. When a sow was feeling affectionate towards her litter she would utter a rapid series of soft grunts. 159 went on like a machine gun until I had made it quite clear to her that I was prepared to accept her apology.

The reaction of sows to their litters was different in almost every case. Number Eleven, on whom George had devoted so much time and energy, turned out to be a thoroughly nasty bit of work. The first time that she farrowed she produced twelve piglets and managed to guzzle four of them before I realised what was going on. I was farrowing three sows at the time and could not understand why the numbers of her newborn pigs seemed to fluctuate every time I came to see how she was doing. I thought I must be counting rather worse than usual until I caught her redmouthed. It was an extremely sinister sight. She would produce a pig and then roll over onto her belly and sit motionless while it crawled up to where it hoped it would find a teat. Then she would strike like a cobra and, with a few smacks of the lips, the piglet would be gone.

In subsequent farrowings we filled her full of happy drugs

and stuck an old gumboot over her jaws. She hallucinated quite peacefully for the first twenty-four hours of her motherhood by which time her litter had become a normal part of life's rich pageant and she accepted them without fuss.

One of the best mothers turned out to be the pig that had survived the fire. The five piglets she dropped after she had recovered from the worst of her ordeal were her first litter. When she caught sight of her first piglet the average sow would become quite excited and start nuzzling it, making the little grunting, 'woofling' noise. This gilt woofled with love and affection for as long as her litter was on her. The 'woofle' cannot be an easy noise for the pig to make as she cannot keep it up for long without breaking down into a paroxysm of coughs. The gilt coughed herself hoarse and eventually lost her voice completely.

My brother had an encounter with this animal when he came and stayed for the weekend. We were moving her from the farrowing house to one of the multi-suckling pens. She went in first and my brother carried over a couple of piglets to join her. He entered the pen with the squealing young and the mother, enraged at this mistreatment of her hard-won offspring, went for him. My brother was under the impression that the sow was trying to get at the piglets to eat them, having listened to one too many of my horror stories.

There followed another of those scenes which became quite familiar on the farm of Man being pursued by enraged pig. She followed him out of the pen and across the garden at high speed, while he was prepared to lay down his life in defence of the piglets should she catch up with him. It was only when he tripped and dropped one that he perceived the misunderstanding between himself and the pig. The sow behaved like a mother rather than a monster and the contretemps restored itself.

Some sows could really make a meal of farrowing by straining away and groaning over periods of twelve hours or more. At the other extreme, we had a sow who would drop her litter in forty-five minutes while nonchalantly chewing straw. One gilt, over the four late-night hours during which she farrowed, lost all her concentration, stood up in the crate and squealed if she was left alone. This sometimes happened and although it was very flattering to feel wanted by the stock, it was a bloody nuisance at 4 am. When this animal came to squeeze out her first pig, she let out an ear-shattering scream. All the pigs on the farm, lying peacefully in a deep sleep, leapt to their feet and started to grunt and squeal in consternation and sympathy. I left the farrowing house to try to reassure them but, judging by their reaction to me, they seemed to think that I must have put the thumbscrews on her.

The sows usually reacted to my appearance with equanimity and a vague interest, just in case I might be carrying any food. Younger pigs treated anyone and anything as a potential threat, probably because it was quite fun to do so. If anybody hove into sight in front of a store pen or if the cat jumped on their wall there would come the explosive alarm bark from one of the inmates followed by a scampering rush to form a pile of suspicious piglets against the back wall. This would gradually melt as its members peeled off to come to investigate the reason for the alarm when it proved to be of no immediate danger.

One of my mistakes was investing a large sum of money in an all-weatherproof oilskin suit, complete with sou'wester. I first put this on when going to check the sow yards on a miserable winter evening. There was one sow mooching by one of the pen gates and she spotted me coming. She gave one incredulous horrified look at the sinister black shiny figure that was approaching and alarm-barked. There was the sound as of a regiment of heavy cavalry at the charge and two walls at the back of the yards collapsed under the impact of a dozen mature animals smashing into them as they tried to escape. In vain did I take off the sou'wester and say, 'Look, it's only me.' I had to take off the whole suit before they were reassured and I was never able to wear the damn thing again if I was after co-operation from the pigs.

The most serious point of conflict that we had with the sows was when moving them from the farrowing house into the multi-suckling pens. Initially I was rather uneasy about farrowing crates. In some circles it was fashionable at the time to be against the war in Vietnam, in favour of legalising cannabis and against farrowing crates which were emotively called the Iron Maidens. These days, it is still cannabis, a different kind of Iron Lady and nuclear power. The Iron Maiden would have been taken out of the lexicon at once had the objectors ever visited my farm. I always had to ensure that the doors of the farrowing house were firmly shut if any sows were in the yard. Otherwise they would barge past me and straight in, making a beeline for the nearest empty crate where they would settle down and refuse to emerge without considerable persuasion from any blunt instrument that I had to hand.

Putting them into the crates when they were due to farrow was, then, no problem; getting them out was not so easy. They would have had a few weeks of indolence surrounded by their loving brood. Food would be brought to them in bed and there would be none of that heart-stopping terror when they sprinted towards the feeders and found that their usual place had been already occupied by another sow. Also, thanks to my attempts at insulation, it was a bit warmer than the yards and there was plenty of straw to play with. It was not surprising that they would prefer captivity to comparative freedom.

After we had managed to extricate them from the crates, the next problem was to drive them, often protesting and squealing, towards the multi-suckling pens. Moving sows about was not usually too difficult as the yards where they lived were enclosed by a containing wall and, if I had remembered to shut the gate, they were not able to run very far. The suckling pens were outside this complex and once out in the wide blue yonder, problems could arise.

Some animals behaved admirably. They would wander gently in the right direction, occasionally stopping to perform a bit of gentle weeding in the gaps and holes in the concrete of the yard, and then go straight into their new pen without a murmur. They were in the minority. There were those that considered it an act of lunacy to travel in a straight line towards the dragon country that lay beyond the sow yards and would have to be dragged, protesting furiously. If your guard relaxed for a second, they would double back to the yard and dive thankfully back into a farrowing crate and the procession would have to start again.

The worst of the lot were the runners. Once this brand of pig had been extricated from her crate she would be out of the farrowing house like a rocket. By the time that I had reached the door I would see her tail-end disappearing down the drive towards the bus stop or the slag heaps. The sows, as well as being stronger than me, were a good deal faster and I could spend hours chasing after them. Once I managed to grab the tail of one of these animals as she careered down the lane. The inhabitants of the bungalows, sipping their mid-morning cups of cocoa, were now entertained by my bouncing down the middle of their road on my behind with the sow dodging her way between the hearses on their way to the crematorium.

One of these runners spent twenty four hours clambering up to the summit of one of the slag heaps and skiing her way down again. I chased after her for a couple of hours but gave up after I fell into a hole that seemed to be the local dump for waste oil. She was waiting in the sow yards at feeding time the next day.

Any problems that we had with the yard and multi-suckling system were brought on by the inherently nasty nature of the pigs. Introducing three or four sows into a pen would lead to half an hour of fights before they had worked out their various levels in the pecking order. Next they would dung in all the wrong places and see what could be easily destroyed. We would bring their hungry piglets to them and as the sows would be feeling uncomfortably full of milk they would all settle down to give suck and peace would at last reign.

The fighting could be even worse in the yards. We had one sow who aborted her litter for no obvious reason. We called in the vet who diagnosed arthritis, which seemed an odd cause of

97

her symptom. He advised me to isolate her and fed her on kippers. Wondering vaguely if he was trying to take the piss out of me, I did as I was told and fed her a stream of kippers and finnan haddock. Not surprisingly she went off this diet and the vet rediagnosed her disease as pneumonia. She had that for a week or so and the vet was just about to opt for beri-beri and housemaid's knee when she decided to die. The post mortem revealed that she had had a massive blood clot inside her uterus, the most likely explanation for which was that another sow had had a fight with her and had trodden on her.

The yard system was very unkind to the odd sow that had to be introduced into a pen full of strangers. Strangers were pigs that had not had nose to nose contact within the previous few days. The incomer would be bullied unmercifully. I found a rather bizarre solution to the problem in the shape of an air pistol from my youth. I discarded the weapon as a child when the sparrows and starlings whose blood I was after failed to drop dead when I shot them. They would instead look thoughtfully up at the sky and curse any loose-bowelled pigeon that might be passing overhead.

When a young sow was introduced into a strange yard I would keep an eye open until I had spotted the main bully. I would then pepper her with the air pistol whenever she started to beat up the incomer. After half a dozen shots the bully would become dimly aware that her victim had some strange and effective means of retaliation and was best left strictly alone. This gave the new pig time to settle in and pluck up the courage to stand up for herself.

Piggin' Politics!

In early days our litter numbers were a good deal lower than they ought to have been. This was caused by more than one factor. Our service technique was pretty lousy, to wit George's performance with Number Eleven. Also the boars lived with groups of sows that were supposed to be already pregnant. If one of them was not, when we pulled the boar out for one of his official services in front of the feeders, he might have already worn himself into a frazzle on his penpal. The other main problem stemmed from the fact that Ted's herd had not been in the first flush of youth when we took it over. They were a bunch of geriatrics, in fact, and this was not helped by the fire in which seven of the animals which died had been gilts expecting their first litters.

The problem of how and when to dispose of elderly sows was one that we never really solved. There were plenty of eager takers. The local knacker would take them off our hands and give us a fiver in return. The markets always seemed to raise three times as much for anyone else's pigs as our own. We had a sentimental attachment to our sows and felt that it was the height of ingratitude to turn them into catfood after many years of long and faithful service. The pig was insufficiently fluffy to qualify for a happy retirement under the 'cuddly bunny' syndrome. Cantankerous and useless old donkeys had their sanctuaries and there seemed to be endless old ladies leaving their money to ponies and cats; but my poor old sows were only good to feed them. Still harsh economics were harsh economics and the bank manager would not have appreciated groups of pensioned old sows eating their way into his profits.

We eventually found a local butcher who miraculously transformed raddled old sows into juicy joints of pork for the delectation of his customers, and for a time this seemed to be a more honourable path to heaven than being eaten by moggies. There was always the problem of deciding when a sow was actually due for the Happy Rootling Grounds. Should she be allowed two bad litters, or only one? We tended to compromise and sows that we liked stood a better chance of survival than the others.

Number 11 was given the chop as soon as she produced less than ten piglets. Whether she had actually produced twelve and had already eaten two, I was not sufficiently interested to find out. On the other hand, 159 alias 28, who was such a sweetie and would sometimes even join us for walks amid the rural slum that surrounded us, dribbled on producing fours and fives for quite some time before she was enheavened.

Normally, when there was a sow that we wanted to dispose of, I would telephone the butcher to alert him and drop the animal into the local abattoir on a Sunday when it would cease to be my responsibility. The butcher then took over and paid me the money a few days later with a deduction for what he called insurance. The system worked well enough, until one Sunday afternoon I reached the gates of the abattoir and found that they were shut.

I found a call box and discovered that the drover who was normally there to greet me had dropped dead in the pub the preceding night and there had not yet been found anyone to replace him. I was advised to take the sow home again and return with her the following day when there would be a few more people to take charge of the animal. When I got back to the car I found that the trailer, which had never been particularly robust, had been transformed into a neat heap of firewood by its cargo and she was now gallivanting up and down a nearby street with a crowd of children and a football.

I had no string or rope handy to secure her and raising a haulier at *News of the World* and nookie time on a Sunday afternoon was beyond the resources of the call box. With the help of the children, who considered the project immense fun, I loaded the sow into the back of the estate car and took her and the remains of the trailer - two wheels and a chassis - back home. The sow was elderly and very large, in fact the sort of passenger that would bring a policeman's blood pressure up to dangerous levels.

Her initial act was to turn and look out of the back window. This meant that she was presenting her bum to me which gave her the opportunity to piddle half a gallon down the back of my neck. She became interested in the passers-by and smashed the glass of one of the windows so that she could have a better look. She then got lonely and decided to come over to join me in the front seat and could be dissuaded with only the greatest of difficulty.

All in all, the back seat of a car cannot be recommended as the ideal place in which to transport sows. The journey was made worthwhile by the expressions on the faces of pedestrians. Being black, she was not immediately recognised as being a pig by the general public. Moreover, you do not expect to see a bloody great sow lolling in the back of a motor car on a Sunday afternoon. She blotted her copybook at one point when we drew up at some traffic lights and a Ford full of suburban family drew up beside us. She stuck her head out of the window and started to grunt at the children in the back seat adjacent. It was when she tried to break in through their window that they started to scream, at which point the lights turned green and I hurried off. Once out in the open country she found that she could achieve an interesting rocking motion by swaying from side to side. The car would lurch towards the ditch and, as I compensated, it would lurch in the other direction towards the oncoming traffic. All in all, I had rarely been more happy to get safely home.

There was a sequel to this. The sow went back to the abattoir on Monday and was seen no more. A few days went by. I did not receive the cheque for her remains so I telephoned the butcher to whom I had sold her to find out what the hitch was.

'Good afternoon,' he said.

'Hullo,' I said. 'About that sow that I had dropped in to the slaughterhouse for you the other day. How did she get on?'

'Hang on. That's Mr Robertson, isn't it? I'll just check. Oh yes. She killed out at quite a good weight.'

'Good. I'm pleased to hear it. I haven't received a cheque from you yet.'

'Haven't you? That's bad. I'll see if I can find out why.' He put down the telephone and I could hear him leafing through some papers on his desk before he picked up the receiver again. 'Ah yes. She was condemned as being unfit for human consumption.'

'Why?'

'I don't know but the meat inspector must have had good reason. I'm sorry,' he continued cheerfully. 'That means that you don't get a penny for her.' He put the telephone down and I quietly seethed. He was getting the sows cheap and I had understood that he was the one who was meant to be carrying that risk, not me. I dug out one of the slips of paper that had accompanied a previous cheque from him. '*Less deductions of £3 for killing charges and insurance.*' Insurance! That sounded interesting. I telephoned up his assistant.

'I've just been looking through my books and I see that you deducted a sum for insurance from a cheque you sent me for a sow that I had sold you. What's that insurance for?'

'Oh er, it's in case the carcass gets condemned. If it's insured it means that you still get your money.'

'I see,' I said, all sweetness and light. 'Would you transfer me to your boss, please.' I got through to the boss. 'Robertson here again. According to your assistant, the sum of money that you deduct from my cheque each time goes for insuring against the possibility of the animal being condemned. I would like my money, please.'

'Ah,' said this pillar of the local community, thinking fast. 'The insurance, it's not for the whole carcass. It's just for the head and the guts. They are the parts of the animal that are most often condemned, you see.'

You miserable bastard, I thought. There was nothing on the slip of paper that said for precisely what portion of the pig's anatomy insurance would be paid, so I did not think that there was very much I could do about it.

'That's a great shame,' said I.

'Isn't it.' said he.

'In that case, you can just send me a cheque for the value of the head and guts, if that was all that was covered by your insurance policy.'

'Ah,' he said. I had realised that the 'ah' would presage him saying something that would not be to my advantage, 'There's a bit of a problem there. You see I deduct the money to pay for the insurance off the money that I owe you....' He paused.

'So?'

'Well, because the animal was condemned, it means that I won't be paying you and so I won't be deducting any money to pay for their insurance. So you see she was not insured.'

I checked with my solicitor but there was nothing I could do about it. That gentleman joined a select group whom I have encountered in my life whom I would kick extremely hard if I had come face to face with them in a dark alley. After that, we sent our sows to a farmer deep in the Welsh mountains, and where they finally ended up I never found out.

With some of the older sows going out one end, we had to replace them with younger pigs at the other. We had bought some young Saddleback gilts along with the rest of the herd from Ted. By the time that these had reached maturity we had decided to replace the purebred sows with crossbred to improve the quality of our weaners. A farmer who was starting up a herd of pigs bought sixteen of the gilts, leaving us only three which were to plug a gap until the crossbreds were ready. We found out later that those pigs came to a miserable end. The farmer went on the booze for a couple of weeks and, when he came to again, his entire herd had died of thirst and starvation. Apart from the agony of the animals, it seems incomprehensible that anyone could allow a few bottles of Scotch to rob him of stock worth several thousand pounds.

The replacement crossbred gilts were to be a combination of Duke's work and my own. The benefits of artificial insemination seemed obvious. Only semen from the very best boars was miraculously induced into little bottles for distribution round the country's pig farms. By using semen of this quality I was buying boars worth thousands of pounds rather than eighty pounds, which was the most that I ever paid for a boar of my own. I bought myself a large rubber penis and set to it. The technique was quite simple to learn. Like the boar, the AI inseminator stuffs his catheter up the back-end of the selected sow, screws it in and waits for ages until the sow suddenly decides that the time is right and sucks the semen from the little bottle that is fixed to the other end of the instrument.

The boar has a much easier time of it than a man. The boar merely has to lean on the sow for twenty-odd minutes and let nature take its course. Presumably he enjoys himself quite a bit at the same time. The man has to ensure first that his sow is on heat which means jumping on its back to find out whether it will stand still. If she is, he then has to fend off the farm boars until the postman brings the semen. Once he has inserted his penis (rubber), he has to ensure that it and the bottle are always at the correct angle which means staying bent double with his eyes on the rear end of the sow which, like most views, tends to pall after a bit.

It became even worse when the sow got bored and started to wander off. If she tried that game with the boar on board, she would have her face beaten in. The inseminator does not have this freedom of assault and has to follow her at a swift crouch clutching determinedly to her tail with one hand and steadying the bottle with the other. If the lover of the pig is more than five feet tall it plays hell with the spine.

The sows were never really convinced of my abilities as a lover and produced some pretty lousy litters to prove it. Where I may have failed was in my attempts to withstand the ever-present temptation to give the bottle a surreptitious squeeze when I thought I was not looking and squirt the stuff into the sow rather than wait for her pleasure. I found twenty minutes of making love to a pig a very long time. If my wife could be so lucky.

The first batch of ten crossbred gilts were a combination of

Duke's work and my own and we gave them the little waddling boar, Ron. Both Ron and the gilts were rather young to start breeding and we left them to gambol away the summer and grow a bit larger. Inevitably, when we decided that it was time that they started breeding we found that nature's judgement had overruled our own and that all ten of them were already in pig. Ron's waddle was rather more pronounced than before.

We had no idea of the dates that these gilts were due to farrow and found it very difficult to make a guess based on the degree of swelling round their teats. Unlike sows, the udders of gilts do not swell with milk before they produce their first litter. Which was a pain, as the early warning could be very useful to the less than efficient farmer who had made a balls-up of his farrowing dates. Some we managed to put into the farrowing house in time. Others beat us to it in the sow yards.

We had a disaster with a batch of nine in-pig gilts that I bought at auction to fill a gap before more of Duke's offspring came through. They were of impeccable pedigree - rubber penis out of champion sow. The owner of the farm had seen the way the economic winds were blowing about four months before it turned into a gale and was selling up completely and retiring to Bournemouth. That was one of the factors that added to the uncertainty of pig farming. Over the course of a couple of years pigs can move from profit to loss and back again. It makes any attempt to forecast income in the future utterly impossible. Every time that the cycle moves down, the inefficient farmers go bankrupt and when it goes up another bunch of inefficient hopefuls start up.

The auction was the first time that I had seen any of my fellow pig farmers *en masse*. I discovered that they do not find it necessary to affect the flat caps and stout brown brogues that are worn by other members of the farming fraternity and, apart from the faint miasma of pigshit that hung over them, one would have found it hard to pick them out in a crowd.

Most of the attendants at the auction seemed to have come just for a social poke around and were not buying anything, which allowed me to buy nine sows at a fairly reasonable price out of the ring formed by the spectators. It was a very hot summer day with lots of wasps buzzing about and you could follow their progress by the flurries of waving hands and hats rippling through the crowd. Proceedings came to a complete standstill two or three times when a wasp landed on the back of a sow that was in the ring. There would be complete silence as we would all stare, fascinated, wondering if the pig would be stung and, if so, how she would react. One wasp landed on a boar as it was being led round the ring and the audience melted backwards rather hurriedly as it had no desire to discover the reactions of a boar at too close quarters.

The statistics of the herd were read out by the auctioneer before the sale started - average number of pigs reared per sow and the like - and were greeted by howls of disbelief from the audience. He read out the history of each sow before it was sold; each one seemed to be better than the last and the raucous incredulity of the audience grew and grew. The vendor became quite upset and started to trade insults with the crowd, especially when the spectators showed their disapproval by refusing to bid for a particularly scruffy pig that was supposed to have reared sixteen piglets in each of its litters.

Many bidders were mesmerised by the gleaming beauty of the twin meal hoppers and there was some spirited bidding for them. The status symbol of the dairy farmer is his high silage tower which proclaims his superiority over the surrounding countryside. Pig farmers do their best to emulate by buying high meal hoppers to show that they, too, are no slouches when it comes to capital investment. The arable farmer just breeds bigger and newer tractors and combines. The buzz went round the crowd during the bidding that the price these hoppers had reached was more than they cost when new. The two who were vying for them melted away into the crowd and, to the fury of the auctioneer and the vendor, they had to be put up again and fetched a couple of hundred pounds less.

These nine pigs were hopeless. Only one was retained after the first litter. Most of them showed some congenital weakness after farrowing and never raised themselves from their confinement beds. One produced thirteen piglets, all of which were deformed and died within a couple of days. Another had the cheek to go through her entire pregnancy, decide to farrow with much groaning and sighing with lots of milk on her - and produced nothing but a series of almighty farts. We revenged ourselves on her by putting her in the deepfreeze, and very tasty she turned out to be.

That was the last batch of pigs that we bought from outside. A pig that had been reared on the premises could turn up its toes just like any other, but it did not leave such an unpleasant hole in the pocket and the accounts. At least its cost is spread over several months and, if you try hard enough, you can fool yourself into hiding its cost entirely.

Apart from the cost of meal, the cost of disease was always the biggest drain on our pocket. At times it seemed as though we were waging a constant battle against the insane desire of our stock to be dead. The animals that were always the most enthusiastic about death were the young piglets. Quite frequently at parturition there would be one animal that would turn up its toes after a quick, jaundiced look at the world. If it could not actually be bothered to summon up the energy to die immediately, it certainly would not make the effort to find a teat and we would end up with another Gruntle-type monster on our hands.

These little brutes paraded through the oven of the Aga in a never-ending stream. They were always very nearly dead when they were brought in - otherwise they would have been left on the sow. If they were extremely very nearly dead, they would graduate to the Aga via a washing-up bowlful of hot water to warm them up. This would be followed by half an hour in a moderate oven. If it was summer and the Aga out, then half an hour at gas mark 4. By then, the little bastard would either have made it and be dead or else be fit enough to dominate our lives for the next few weeks through its constant demand for a bottle.

The piglets that did not travel across the Styx by this route would remain with their mothers and wait to get the trots. One of the mistakes I made was in having only one farrowing house which was never empty and was never able to be rested and disinfected properly to prevent a build-up of disease. The odd fire certainly helped, but it was a rather drastic method of sterilisation. When the dreaded *E. coli* bug struck, the litter members would all get the trots and start to die as swiftly as they could. Then it became a case of pumping antibiotics down their throats as quickly as possible as a counter-measure. In times of great mortality we would even summon the vet who would look at the victims of the plague and reassure me in his best litter-side manner. One of his diagnoses about a litter of piglets, spraying the farrowing house from their arses, was that perhaps it was due to the sows getting old.

Between these waves of disease our piglet mortality was very low which, I suppose, is a bit like describing someone as being in perfect health apart from his terminal case of cancer. After the rosebed became full and any attempt to dig further graves resulted in a dull clang as the spade hit a biscuit tin, the departed piglets ended up on the midden. It should have been a simple process. I would find a dead piglet in its creep and remove it. It became more complex because it was not all that easy to decide when a piglet was actually dead. A small pig could fall into a sleep so deep that it was virtually impossible to arouse it. I would come on this limp object, pick it up, give it a thump and dunk it in a bucket of water and decide that in the absence of any response, heartbeat or breathing, it was probably dead. I would then chuck it on the midden only to have it wake up as soon as it hit the ground and clamber, squealing, back down to have me sheepishly return it to its mother.

One piglet took this affliction a stage further. When the sow lay down to suckle it would come tearing out of the creep with its litter mates to grab a teat and collapse in a deep twitching sleep half-way to its goal. It must have been highly frustrating for it. I even checked with the vet in case it was suffering from fits or some other complaint; but no, it just liked its kip.

The death of piglets was the most infuriating aspect of pig farming as it was such a waste. A dead pig would not arouse feelings of pity in my breast because the poor little soul had passed on, but acute irritation that it should be so spineless as to give up and thus cheat me out of twenty pounds, or whatever the going rate might be. This would be compounded by a sense of failure. Nature and the sow had done their bit in presenting me with a litter of twelve piglets and any deaths on the way to maturity should have been prevented by better conditions or better care.

The sows were rather healthier than their young which was just as well because when they were off colour it was very difficult to find out why. I once caught the vet in an unguarded moment and he told me why he found the pig such a hard animal to treat. It was oblong, fat and had few interesting protuberances on which he could get his hands. The thick layer of fat made it virtually impossible for him to hear the actions of heart and lungs and prevented him from feeling any internal organs and finding fault there. As a result, he tended to treat every sow with a temperature with the same shot of broad-spectrum antibiotic and hoped that would cure any ailment that it might be suffering from. After listening to that I obtained my own supply of drugs and did the jabbing myself with no noticeable increase in pig mortality.

Over the course of our span on the farm we must have had about 115 sows and out of that number, four adult animals died on us, all in the same week. That figure excludes, of course, those that went up in smoke. They all died of entirely unrelated causes. George was the first to go, his digestion having finally collapsed under the strain he put on it. Another sow died of the blood clot on her uterus; one died of heart failure and another after a prolapse.

The knacker was quite sympathetic when he came to pick up George. The heart failure case was in a multi-suckling pen where she had sixteen piglets on her. There were two other sows in with her and, fortunately, her litter was about three weeks old and ready to be weaned. The knacker was rather more cheerful that time and was positively affable when he came to collect the blood-clot case. I telephoned him the next day to collect the last victim. She had fallen in her farrowing crate a few days before her litter was due and had started to bleed internally. I switched her to a well-strawed pen by herself but she threw out her uterus and died.

The knacker came on the yard singing 'O What a Beautiful Morning.'

'It's not a matter for rejoicing,' I snarled. He did his best to look contrite.

'Look on the bright side,' he said.

'What bright side?'

'It may be a tragedy for you but one man's meat, etcetera. Every time that one of your pigs drop dead, you call me up and I make some money. Be happy,' he exhorted, ' because you're helping to make me rich.'

My reply was unprintable - even here - but you cannot keep a happy knacker down. He started to winch the corpse of the sow on to his wagon. 'Had a good week, last week,' he said.

'Good for you,' I said discouragingly.

'Made a fortune. Do you know what I picked up?'

'The clap?'

'No. A bloody great whale. The council called me up and there stretched out on the beach was this dirty great thing.....Beginning to stink a bit, mind you.....It was lovely.'

'It sounds delightful.' My interest stirred in spite of myself. 'But what on earth do you do with a dead whale?'

'I sold it for a bomb to a maggot breeder from Bradford.' I shut up after that. After he had gone I went back into the pen to clear up and found a tiny piglet running around. It must have fought its way clear before its mother had died, but without the disease protection provided by her colostrum it died a few hours later.

The problem of savaging only touched us briefly. Pigs are notorious in that they can frequently pick on one of their number and worry away at it until they cause it serious injury or even kill it. We had the odd sow which would absent-mindedly polish off one or two piglets for breakfast but, apart from that, we had only one pen of stores that gave us any worries. For no discernible reason they started to fight amongst themselves when they were about five weeks old. We had a constant stream of battered piglets being ferried to the sickroom to be watched over by the hen and ended up with seven completely earless pigs.

After Dick the fattener had bought them he reported no further trouble. He did occasionally tell us of troubles with our pigs at later stages of growth, usually when we were trying to screw more money out of him and he was countering with reasons why he could not afford to pay it. One of the advantages of the 'blue' crossbred pig is that the dash of Saddleback blood in it makes it rather more docile and phlegmatic than its white contemporaries. One of the reasons is the simple one of having lop ears. If it cannot see what there is to fight, it will not fight.

Too Many Snouts in the Trough!

My conception of the farmer before I had actually joined their ranks was very similar to Landseer's conception of the stag - that of Monarch of his Glen; in my case the hillock amid the slag heaps. He was liable to shoot the odd poacher or rambler who was sufficiently foolish to stray across his domain, would leave vast sums of money to his descendants and vote slightly to the right of Attila the Hun. At intervals he or the NFU as his representatives would appear on television and give the rest of us a good laugh when he tried to plead poverty.

I soon found that, although this may have been true of certain sections of the agricultural community a few decades ago, it had all changed. Just as Landseer had failed to paint in the nasty fat little businessman who was crawling up the other side of the stag's mountain carrying a rifle, so my image failed to include that particularly unpleasant parasite, the bureaucrat. These came in two varieties, the local and the national, and both had considerably more say over my destiny than myself. The tragedy was that, before I became a farmer, I honestly did not object to servants, civil or otherwise. They had their jobs to do like everyone else. Actually meeting them rather soured my impression. The one exception to a blanket condemnation of the whole breed of bureaucrats is the Ministry of Agriculture whose advisory service is staffed by people who seem to want to help the farmer rather than to wrap him up in red tape until he suffocates.

In balmy pre-farming days the full horror of the government department had not really dawned on me. At that time I paid as I earned and so never met the Inland Revenue. VAT had not been invented and our semi was beneath the notice of both the local authority and the Dept. of the Environment. This state of innocence disappeared when I slipped away from the easily controlled regiments of the employed and became a farmer.

The first faint twinge of unease hit me when a rather complex form dropped through the letter box which informed me that

I was the occupier of Holding Number 363/0712/72947 and would I please inform them how many cows and lettuces I possessed and how many of my broad acres were used to grow sugar beet. Having neither cows, lettuces nor any broad acres on which to grow sugar beet nor even, at that time, any pigs, the form was consigned to the wastepaper basket. A little later another form arrived demanding the same information with the menace that unless I replied within seven days, I would be fined five pounds or be transported to Tasman's Peninsula. Like a good citizen I wrote none or zero all over the form and returned it feeling that I had done my bit for Queen and Country.

There was a short lull before another letter dropped through the box saying that my answers were not in accordance with previous information and would I please explain. I wrote back to say that I had no knowledge of their previous information and therefore was unable to explain it. Quick as a flash they riposted with yet another form across which I wrote, 'See Previous Correspondence' and there the matter ended.

'See Previous Correspondence' is a useful standby for emergencies when you are dealing with officialdom. It strikes terror into the heart of the beaurocrat. It insinuates that there has been a letter - a precious piece of paper - that has been lost by him. He will immediately institute a search of all government offices from Aberdeen to Plymouth and, when nothing turns up, will not dare to write again. I have used this device sparingly but with complete success on every occasion it was employed.

The basic trouble about the civil servant is that he has forgotten that he is a servant. We pay him his salary and it is his duty to serve the State, which means we taxpayers, to the best of his ability. Instead he seems to think we should serve him. The worst sinner in that respect that I have yet come across was a horrid little Hitler who worked for the Inland Revenue. To give the organisation its due, since my ghastly encounter they have always treated me with reasonableness and courtesy. But that specimen, along with the butcher who diddled me, is one of that select group of three whom I dearly wish to meet in a darkened alley.

Anyway I, an innocent young pig farmer, received a tax assessment for a large number of pounds. This was the first time that I had ever seen such a document and, highly alarmed, I ran to my accountant for care and protection. He told me to appeal. Apparently the assessment was merely a tactic by the Inland Revenue to force me to produce my accounts so they could work out how much money was actually owed. So the accountant pored over the books for many days and eventually worked something out. Everything appeared to add up; there were not too many glaring anomalies and the end result was an extremely modest profit. Ho Ho. Yet another farmer was trying to pull the wool: but times were hard, I was scarcely an efficient farmer and the modesty of the profit was quite genuine and fully documented.

Everything was put in a large envelope, posted off to the local tax office and the Inland Revenue was forgotten about for another year. It was not to be. The first slight disquiet came in a letter a week or two later. 'Some points have arisen which raise doubts on the adequacy of the accounts submitted.' With all those points and doubts rising like rocketing pheasants I began to become uneasy. He ended, 'You may find that you would prefer to call in the office to discuss these matters.'

'Help,' I said to my accountant. He patted me reassuringly on the head and told me not to worry. He had had thirty years of experience in one of the top London firms of accountants and was not about to start getting worried over queries about a few measly pigs. However, to set my mind at rest, he agreed to come in with me. The letter-writer was young, spotty and exceedingly belligerent. Even the police when the barn went up were prepared to give me the benefit of the doubt and assume that I was innocent until they found evidence that showed otherwise. Not this civil servant.

The questions flowed. Not, 'You bought a boar for £80. From whom did you buy it?' but, 'You claim you bought a boar for £80.' The insinuation throughout was that I was lying, that my accountant was probably lying and that it was up to this seedy knight in shining armour to confront us with the truth. I was baffled and my accountant turned a curious shade of red but managed to control his emotions. We left, seething.

I received another summons to appear before the almighty. This time he wanted all my bank statements for the previous four years and we churned through them item by item. It was not easy to account for a credit of twelve pounds that went in a couple of years earlier, but we did our best. We went through the cash book and my records of litters per sow and on through his closely typed transcript of our previous interview where he tried to catch us out on any inconsistencies.

Letters flowed back and forth and we visited the office again. The breaking point came during a wrangle about a paint brush. I had bought it to whitewash a boar pen but had also used it to paint our downstairs loo. What was the correct split? The brush cost 40p. Was it 25p business and 15p private? My accountant suddenly turned from red to white.

'This is absurd. I see no reason why the time of myself or my client should be further wasted on these trivialities.' He stumped out with myself in attendance.

That was virtually it. I had one more letter from him stating that I had no liability for tax owing to surplus reliefs. The tragedy of the situation was the enormous waste of time and effort. Even assuming the worst, that my accounts were the biggest fairy story since Hans Christian Andersen, there was still no possible way that I could have hauled my income up to a sufficiently high level to have given the taxman a worthwhile return for his time. The only possible explanation for the performance was that we were landed with a new man and our file was given to him so that he could cut his teeth on a real case which was sufficiently unimportant for him to do little damage.

There was a sequel. Some years later I contacted my new tax office about some query or other which needed a consultation of my file. I mentioned to the clerk that I had had a bit of difficulty in the past and asked if there was anything interesting on my file. She looked at it and then burst into shrieks of laughter. I have been rather worried ever since.

The taxman was undoubtedly the most dangerous hunter stalking the agricultural monarch's glen, but he had his imitators. The VAT man was one. He was a fairly recent innovation who conducted his business by computer. VAT heralded its arrival with a dazzling display of paper pyrotechnics. Fat envelopes thudded through millions of letter boxes bearing thrilling information such as that coffins were liable to pay the full rate of tax, while coffin fittings were exempt, or it may have been zero rated. They say there is a subtle difference. Thousands of farmers learned to bounce all these reams of paper straight into the bin, since the only piece of relevant information was that food production was not taxed and we all knew that already.

The Customs people had the bright idea of making the taxpayer the tax collector as well, and so every month all those registered fill in forms and send them off with their cheques to the Customs and Excise computer at Southend. The farmer, like everyone else, was supposed to fill in his form but he got money back from the computer rather than giving it.

Early on we decided that it was a bit daft to fill in our form each month to receive the miserable fiver or so that was all that our way of farming could generate. It was extra work for HM Customs and ourselves. So, as recommended, we opted for three-monthly returns instead. We sent a polite letter off to the computer. It ignored the communication and remorselessly continued to churn out forms for us. We chucked them in the bin and sent it another nice letter. The computer became annnoyed and began to issue threats. Another of our ultimate weapons in the fight against bureaucracy was invoked.

Computers do not understand the 'See Previous Correspondence' stratagem. They have a theory of their own that they cannot make mistakes so cannot have lost anything. You cannot fit the words 'See Previous Correspondence' into one of the little boxes on their forms and the machines cannot read anything that does not have a box round it. We sent it a letter saying that, unless it minded its manners, we would write to our MP. Of course actually writing to your MP never achieves anything more than a bland reply on House of Commons writing paper, but the threat works wonders. The last thing any civil servant or any civil service computer wants is to have his dirty little arbitrary ways investigated by the standard-bearers of democracy.

Within forty-eight hours we had a real live VAT man on the farm, complete with yellow sports car, apologising profusely for his machine's bad manners. All was sweetness, light and quarterly forms.

After that, ourselves and the VAT men got on reasonably well until they decided that we owed them about thirty pounds. We had sold a trough or something and had neglected to charge the buyer VAT as was apparently our duty. We received a visit from a civil servant full of righteous indignation who proceeded to comb through our accounts for evidence of malpractice. We VAT payers are supposed to preserve receipts for three years so that they can be checked and - miracle of miracles - all our receipts were there and relatively intelligible.

'Very good,' said the VAT man. 'It's always a pleasant surprise on these investigations when everything is in order. Now let's do the arithmetic.' He did the arithmetic with me looking on. Watching an expert adding up a column of figures is an awe-inspiring sight. I also find it rather soothing because it is an ability I do not covet in the slightest. He ended up with two separate figures, and sat back. 'That looks as if you owe us thirty pounds,' he said happily.

I pointed at the other figure. 'You owe me sixty.'

He looked a little worried. 'Yes, I can't understand that. It must be a mistake.' He produced some paper from his black briefcase. 'According to our records, the computer issued a payable instrument for that amount some months ago. So it must have been received by you.

'But you have been through my bank statements which prove that I have never received the money and received no payment advice from your computer. You opened the envelopes and checked the slips yourself.' Lamentably, I found VAT so boring that, although I preserved the envelopes they sent me, I could never summon up sufficient interest to open them and see what they contained. So there could have been no deceit or tampering with them to explain the anomaly.

'If the computer issued instructions for a payment, it follows that it must have been sent and received by you.'

'But it wasn't and I didn't.'

'But it must have been.'

'But it wasn't,' I repeated gently. The certainties of the man's world seemed to be crumbling.

'This is most extraordinary.' The key to understading the mind of a beaurocrat is that his reality is found only inside the inflexible prose of his rule book. Anything that cannot be correlated to that prose cannot exist. 'It seems,' he said, with a brave effort, 'that there may possibly have been a small inexactness.'

'I'm pleased you admit it.'

'I didn't admit anything,' he said hurriedly, a film of sweat breaking out on his forehead. 'I said "may" and "possibly." Anyway, I would like a cheque for thirty pounds.'

'I would like you to give me one for sixty pounds.'

He looked surprised. 'Oh, I can't give you a cheque for sixty pounds. In due course the computer will issue you with a payable instrument.'

'In that case, I will give you a cheque after I have received mine.'

'I am afraid that is not possible. I must have your cheque now.'

'How about if we write to the computer and tell it to knock my thirty off the sixty pounds that it owes me. It would save me issuing a separate cheque.'

He gave a deprecating laugh. 'No, I'm afraid that is just not possible. The system could not possibly cope with a transaction like that.'

'My system cannot cope with a transaction like the one you suggest.' 'You have no alternative,' he said sweetly. 'Ultimately there are sanctions which will force you.'

'But that is absurd and unjust. Why should I pay interest because your oversized abacus makes a balls-up?'

He did not even bother to answer that or my threat to sue the Dept. of Customs and Excise through the civil courts. He just sat patiently, tapping the royal monogram on his briefcase until I got my chequebook.

The Ministry of Agriculture, on the other hand, is the maverick amongst government departments as far as the farmer is concerned. Where they differ is that they really seem to want to help rather than see you behind bars. In fact they must be responsible for increasing output to such an extent that it almost cancels out the amount that other departments succeed in depressing it.

Like all of the Civil Service, it had the tendency to believe that the act of issuing a piece of paper was an achievement in itself. It tended towards garishly printed leaflets, advising of strange diseases that might break out in my oil-seed rape, cows and sheep. These were pinned up in the outside privy but the Ministry also produced advisers. These advisers come in all shapes and sizes and provide a rich seam of expertise on every conceivable agricultural subject in which the farmer can dig to the benefit of both his pocket and the community. The Ministry is unique in that its servants appear capable of tailoring their minds and actions to meet a given situation as opposed to trying to squeeze the situation so that it would fit into the rule book. I have even heard one or two of them admit that they were wrong.

The local authority servants can have almost as much power to disrupt your peace and independence as the national servant but, being locally based, they can never quite achieve the remote, soulless inefficiency of central government although they try very hard. We had dealings with them on several occasions - when we wanted to erect dog kennels, when we wanted an improvement grant for the house and when the Public Health inspector came to call. We learned very early on that such visits should not be encouraged.

The clue was given by the man who came to see if the house was eligible to receive an improvement grant. At that stage we had not yet bought any pigs which probably saved us a great deal of grief. The man wandered round the house by himself and then disappeared. Alarmed in case he had fallen down one of the mine shafts that honeycombed the substructure of the hill, I went to investigate and found him rooting round the drains in the far corner of the yard. Such people cannot keep away from drains. He looked a little guilty, but said that he was just making sure that they were adequate for the premises.

The application for the erection of the kennels brought out a number of these drain fetishists from the local council to examine the site and resulted in a letter telling us that we should transfer from cesspit drainage to the main sewer. We disobeyed their advice which seems to have riled them and they sent out the Public Health Inspector. He was just dropping in to see if everything was in order. Yes, everything was fine and I was a bit busy, so if he wouldn't mind..... Oh no, I wasn't to mind him. He would just wander round a bit and have a look by himself.

I closeted myself in a building and kept an eye on him through the door. He first went into our neighbour's field to examine our cesspit. The lid was well overgrown so he could not raise it. He went to the downhill side and I almost emerged to advise him against such rashness. He disappeared up to his thighs in the rich, fruity bog that winked and wallowed under its thick covering of nettles. I watched him succeed in struggling out after about ten minutes and squelching his way back to the car where he kept a change of clothing. This sort of thing was obviously a hazard of his trade.

He next went into the yard and, with the fixed smile on his face of the man who is truly happy, knelt down beside all the inspection pits and scrutinised the drains. I gave him fifteen minutes before I emerged from my shed and shooed him towards the car. He said that he was quite satisfied but that there were a couple of things that he would like to think about. I asked him what sort of things; but he told me not to worry and that he might drop me a line.

He dropped me a ruddy great book, the gist of which was that, following a complaint about the smell issuing from the midden, I would have to install slurry tanks to hold all the pig muck. If not, I would end up in Botany Bay as usual. Not having four or five thousand pounds to hand, this was out of the question and so a long and complicated stalling action ensued. This took the form of a series of letters congratulating him on his brilliant suggestion and asking where precisely did he think the tanks ought to be built? Did he think that they might look prettier if the interior was painted blue? Surely I would need even more expensive ones than he suggested? I let things lie fallow for a bit until he began to press again. Then I chopped a hole in the top of the disused petrol tank that lived in the middle of the yard, put a bit of shit in the bottom and pretended that it was the first of my tanks, built at great expense. Could he come to inspect it?

The sight of this filled him with such horror, although he gave me full marks for effort which was all I was after, that he started to design some tanks himself. Eventually he retired and his successor appeared to have taken one look at the voluminous file of correspondence and decided that this was one job that would be more trouble than it was worth to follow through to its conclusion. We had a letter thanking us for our co-operation and that was the last we ever heard of it.

Apart from the intrusive horrors of the public servant, we had generally amicable relationships with outsiders. The meal rep always kept us fully posted about local opinions of our activities. We were hippies for the first few weeks until Bernie moved in and then we became leaders of a criminal syndicate. Next was obviously arsonists and finally, after a couple of friends from

London visited us wearing clothes more appropriate for Chelsea than the slag heaps, we became a nest of poofs. I felt that was a bit hard on my wife.

We had a useful little sideline going by selling porkers to the locals. Where we were, most farmers had already cottoned on to the advantages of selling meat direct to the public without the necessity of going through a butcher, and a mini price war had broken out leaving the meat trade wringing its hands in horror about being 50p per pound further up the price scale.

We always had our steady dozen regular customers who could not be wooed away by other producers. Our hottest trade came at Christmas when the local post office came and bought half a dozen pigs off us which I had had slaughtered earlier in the week. They saved money in a Christmas Club-type fund over the year and one of their vans would turn up with a postbag containing about £200 in silver and coppers which would be emptied all over the office floor. The money turned up in odd corners for months. If we were ever short of a bob or two, all it took was a quick scrabble behind the radiator in the office and you could mine as much as you wanted. Other Christmas regulars included the local garage and the crematorium, who smoked their own hams, and assorted builders who had worked at odd times round the house.

One Christmas it was slightly warmer than it should have been and I had knocked off the pigs rather earlier than I should have done. It was always a traumatic moment, the slaughter. These animals would have been around the farm to fatten up for twice as long as the normal piglets and there were usually two or three which had been hand-reared which the fattener had rejected. The actual visit to the abattoir was fraught with peril as the Meat Inspector seemed to be convinced that I filled the carcasses with arsenic before selling them chop by chop to the general public. I always had to pretend that we ate enormous quantities of pork and kept all the pigs for our own consumption, otherwise he would have refused to let us take them away.

That Christmas I had the usual fracas with the Inspector when I loaded the animals into the back of our tatty estate car. Dead beasties are only allowed to travel inside an enclosed van, presumably to prevent potential customers from getting the horrors when they see their Sunday joint trundling by, looking very dead and pig-like. The corpses were strung up in one of the outbuildings with great care. It was always important to keep them high enough off the ground to prevent the piglets who also lived there from standing on each other's shoulders to grab a quick steak. We also had to use wire rather than twine to suspend them so that the rats would not cut them down. The post office collected their batch quite amicably but the last pig, which was earmarked for the plasterer, had turned a curious shade of green by the time that he came to pick it up. I carefully walked round his car so that he was on the windward side of it and, holding my breath to keep the remarkable pong it was giving off out of my nostrils, I hurriedly dumped it into his boot and slammed it shut. I grabbed his money before he could change his mind and waved him out of the yard. Much to my surprise he came back for another pig the following year and remarked on the really meaty taste of my pigs and their tenderness.

Another of our clients was the gardener. The garden had some excellent flowers and shrubs and was well stocked with plants of every description, particularly weeds which came creeping in from the adjacent orchard. There was a problem with the grey dust which would come drifting in from the slag heaps when the wind was in the north but a combination of marauding pigs and regular doses of paraquat tended to keep most of the weeds and the flowers under control.

Then a dear old man turned up who said that he would be delighted to potter round the flower beds for the opportunity to buy the odd piglet at a reduced price. He would then fatten it up in his back garden for resale. The system could have been very successful because anything that prevented me from having to dig the garden suited me, but he only worked on the morning of the day he came to collect the piglet. He would wander round the lawns and then come into the house to drink some coffee. This took up about three hours and then he would go to select his animal. I became wise to him and pointed him in the direction of the sickroom where he had a choice of either the dying or the dead. He would then shuffle off down the lane with his piglet limping along beside him on a bit of string.

The amateur historian who drove the grocer's van was also a keen pig farmer. While she lectured to me on what I was doing wrong her eyes would dart round the stock, searching for anything that looked as if it might be going cheap and would not actually die on her. She once came to the farm with a rather small pig mixed up with the groceries in the back of her van and asked me to put it to one of the boars. I tucked her piglet under my arm and we strolled over to Duke and compared the size of the two animals. We agreed that we really ought to allow her piglet to grow a little larger than a Pekinese before making the poor thing pregnant.

On another occasion she decided to go mad and buy three pigs from me at one go. These were the boars that had been part of an artificially inseminated litter of eleven. The gilts were being retained for breeding. Since I was the father I was quite proud of them and estimated that their weight was 45lb a piece which would have made their cost ten guineas each. She, being an expert, thought that they weighed a lot less and would I please put them through the scales. I did so with considerable inconvenience while she and her husband watched me running round the pen trying to grab these damn pigs that were not co-operating at all. We found that the pigs averaged exactly 45lb each, which was the only time that I ever reached such an amazingly high standard of accuracy. This impressed the woman considerably but left us back where we had started. They were very good pigs but she was used to paying for crippled dwarfs and she started to bargain with me. Patiently I explained how the pricing system worked. Dick payed me £x per pig and then xp for every lb weight. He would give me ten guineas for each pig so why the hell should I make her a present of a few quid? Then her husband joined in, insinuating that I was trying to rob them. I retired to the midden where they could not follow me and started to move rotting piles of muck around which eventually drove them, coughing, back to the van. According to the meal rep, she retaliated by floating the rumour that I was beating my wife but, by that stage, I was well into being a poof and she failed to make it take.

Another of our festive porkers used to go to the man who kept us in motor mowers. Cutting the grass was the only form of gardening that I could not avoid and we had five different stretches of lawn, all on different levels. In the centre of the yard was the new lawn replacing the demolished barn. Over the midden the grass grew green, smelly and rough. Over the remains of the stone foundations and some of the concrete floors that still remained there was a thin parched-brown covering.

Another lawn was planted with nine apple trees, set at precisely the right distance so that anyone trying to cut the grass became inextricably entangled in their branches. The last backed right onto the orchard where there was a constant traffic of escaping pigs, digging great holes in its surface, and rooting out lumps of coal from the shallow seams. Cutting all that herbage used to take about four wasted hours a week. Since the motor mower is carefully designed so that it breaks down as often as possible, thus boosting the sale of new machines and spare parts, it was very expensive grass as well.

I agreed to sell the motor mower dealer a pig on one of his visits provided we could enter into an agreement. We were to put down twenty-five pounds and he was to contract to keep us in functioning motor mowers for the whole season. If one broke down, he had to come out to repair it within twenty-four hours, otherwise it automatically became our property. The poor man agreed to this scheme; in the first five weeks he had to replace three machines and became extremely depressed. He suggested that we ripped up our lawns and concreted them all over. He next tried to sell us vast quantities of that artificial grass that carpets most of America and requires no maintenance except for a hose-down if the wind had been coming off the slag heaps for more than a couple of days. I was adamant. I liked the deal we had. He reneged in the end by going bankrupt.

Apart from reps, our most regular visitors were lorries delivering things, removing pigs or simply lost. Those carrying loads of straw were normally jockeyed by the simplest drivers. They were used to the nice flat lands of East Anglia where their straw had grown as wheat and barley. The combination of our black alps and the twisty winding lane blocked with a funeral procession often unnerved them completely. One arrived grossly overloaded and became stuck at the bottom of our drive after mounting the verge and demolishing a fir tree placed there to prevent lorries mounting the verge. I gave him a tow with the dumper which provided him with enough extra oomph to allow him to regain the hard surface and had to hurriedly mount the verge myself to avoid him as he roared up the hill, terrified to stop in case he bogged again. I could see what was about to happen, but was powerless to prevent it.

Our three magnificent phases of electricity and the telephone wires crossed the yard at just the right height. He went straight through the telephone cable which snapped like thread. He then hit the electricity wires which gave him a bit more resistance, so he changed down a gear and grunted forward, bringing down the wires and two poles which hissed and spluttered round him. He refused to vacate the cab until I switched off at the mains. I did not explain to him that the wires were coming in and so the only way I could turn them off was by going back to the substation but left him in his cab to ponder upon his idiocy for an hour or two while I strolled down to a telephone box and got on to the authorities. We were without power for a couple of days while the shambles was repaired, and wrapped the litters of piglets in blankets and duvets from our beds to keep them alive and warm.

The meal wagon loaded with 320 bags was a regular monthly caller. He always chose a day when it was pouring with rain to make his delivery, and would sit in the yard looking miserable until I went out to give him a hand. I could never discover whether my purchase of meal meant that the load had only to be delivered to my property or had to be put in the mealhouse. The difference was an hour's wet, hard work.

Actually that driver and I got on very well. Naturally he was yet another expert on pigs and plied me with good advice but, almost uniquely, he did not become cross if I failed to take it.

This driver was the antithesis of the man who had sand kicked in his face. I would pick one of the 56lb bags of meal off his wagon and stagger towards the mealhouse, watched by a squealing George. On the way I would be passed by the wagon driver, running with two bags on one shoulder and one on the other. It was a terrifying exhibition of brute strength. I think he liked me to be there just to chat to him and admire him rather than for any help I may have given.

The driver had one of those fabulous grandmothers who had reared thirty-seven children out of a cardboard box and put them all through Oxford with scholarships. All her life she had bought a pig on New Year's day and spent the next year fattening it up to enormous proportions on kitchen scraps before ceremoniously cutting its throat in her back garden just before Christmas. Apparently she would then have an orgy of cutting, curing and sausage making, and all but the tail would disappear into her larder. I once made a very general enquiry of the lorry driver about the best way to cure a ham as we rather fancied the idea of suspending one or two above the logfire in our living room for a week or two. The recipe that he brought along was written in black ink on what looked like parchment and was full of obscure herbs that could only be found on the top of mountains at full moon on Hallowe'en. Granny even turned up in his cab once, wearing black and giving us tips on the best way to clean out intestines and how to scrape off the maggots if they underwent a poulation explosion.

The most powerful driver of the lot was the man who drove the concrete lorry. In his presence the average farmer is turned into a cringing idiot. The driver is the arbiter of the success of the concrete because if he is not treated as a demi-god he will dump his load in a pile in the middle of the yard and leave the farmer to do a couple of hours' frantic barrowing in order to shift the concrete into the right position before it goes hard. If the farmer wears a smile that is sufficiently ingratiating - or even better looks as if he might tip - then the concrete will be carefully put into the right place and much time and effort will be saved.

Our concreting got off to a flying start because the lorry driver was the brother-in-law of the odd-job man who was helping to lay it. The driver was also the father of ten children under fifteen and his wife had just left him which had led to a hundred per cent increase locally in the number of men applying to have vasectomies. This tragic figure would spend hours manoeuvring his wagon so that it was dropping its concrete in little dribbles into each pothole. This idyll came to an end when the odd-job man took five pounds off his relation at poker one night while the women of the neighbourhood were giving his family their weekly bath. The next time the driver came he left his load on top of a pile of blocks just after we had knocked off for lunch and we did not discover it until it was going hard.

After that I invested in an electric concrete mixer of my own which worked very well and, over six months, I pottered round the yard doing all sorts of little jobs that were too big to be done with the shovel and too small to justify a load of pre-mixed concrete. Then I sold the mixer. That was the only time that I ever made a profit on a piece of equipment. I think the new price was £120 and I wanted to sell it for £90. The local wide boy, Geoff, turned up to buy it with a couple of mates in attendance. He softened me up first by walking round the farm, picking holes in my operating methods. When he had reduced the level of my morale sufficiently, he moved on to the mixer and comprehensively pulled that to pieces and made me an offer of £75. He would not move higher and I was not going lower. He really wanted to buy it and I really wanted to sell it.

'Don't be silly, the motor's clapped. You've been overloading it. It's not worth a penny over seventy-five pounds. Isn't that right, Pete? Dai?'

'Yeah.'

'Yeah.'

'But it works perfectly well and I'm certainly not going to give the damn thing away.'

'Give it away? Look, mate, I'm doing you a favour. Judging by the state of the concrete you've laid, the machine's useless anyway. Isn't that right?'

'Yeah.'

'Yeah.'

'Ninety pounds. Not a penny less.'

'Piss off. Look, I'll put it in my trailer and take it away and give you seventy-five in cash. I can't be fairer than that. Come on lads, let's get it aboard.'

'No, hang on. You're offering seventy-five and I want ninety pounds. That's a difference of fifteen pounds. Why not toss a coin for that?'

'Nah. I'm not sure about that. What do you think, lads?'

'It's worth a try.'

'Yeah. It's not a bad idea.'

'I've got a better idea,' I continued. 'We'll toss the coin; if you win, you can have it for forty pounds and if I win, you pay me a hundred and twenty-five in cash.'

'No chance, mate.'

'Go on, Geoff, that's marvellous.'

'Yeah, Geoff. What an opportunity.'

'No.'

'Come on, Geoff. Where's your bottle? Pete'll be the witness. I'll toss the coin and you can call. It's a great idea, innit Pete?'

'Yeah. You're the one who always says he likes a gamble, Geoff.

You can't back out of this one.'

Dai tossed; Geoff fatally opened his mouth and I won. Pete and Dai roared with delight and put the mixer on the trailer while a tight-lipped Geoff pulled a roll of grubby fivers from his pocket and peeled off twenty-five.

The only other vehicle drivers who were regular were the knackers. As befitting for the area, we were served by many knackers. They eventually came to be categorised with public servants at the bottom of our popularity table. Our usual ghoul was off chasing whales once when I called up a rival firm to come to take away a sow which had gone lame. They arrived in a Land Rover which already contained two dead calves and a porker with both its front legs broken. I gave them the benefit of my opinion which was that they would never manage to get the sow into the Land Rover even when empty and, to the best of my knowledge, it was illegal to transport dead and alive animals in the same vehicle.

They reckoned that they knew best and grabbed the sow and tried to lift it into the back. Not surprisingly, the sow, which weighed 500lb, resisted and they spent a quarter of an hour chasing her round the yard before giving up. During this performance, the porker which had already been on the vehicle fell out on the concrete and let out a series of ear-shattering screams which drove every other pig on the farm into a frenzy. I eventually intervened and threw them out, threatening to call the police and the RSPCA if they ever dared set foot in the yard again.

Life, the Universe and.....Snakes

A deep and powerful love of money may not be recommended by St Paul, but since we spend most of our waking moments working in order to collect the stuff, it must be quite a common affliction. I was and am very fond of it but found it hard to gather in large quantities as a pig farmer. Never having been in business for ourselves, we even found it difficult to discover if we were making a reasonable living or not. As a salaried worker, I could work out monthly outgoings as compared with the incomings and aim to end up with a neat sum equalling zero at the end of the day. If I came up with a minus, then we would cut down on booze and fags over the next month. If the figure was zero plus, then we could afford cigars instead.

With a fluctuating overdraft it was not so easy. The bank manager was rather fond of having me produce estimates and projections but we worked out our cash flows and targets and missed them with monotonous regularity. The trouble was that during our first eighteen months in the business the value of each piglet sold went up by 37.5 per cent but the cost of the meal that we pumped into them rose by 130 per cent. The bank manager found these charges rather alarming, and so did I.

We had even more trouble than him in interpreting the bank statements that he sent to us each month. We did some costings with the firm that sold us our meal. The rep would work out our levels of pigs sold per sow per year and the amount of cake that it cost us to keep them alive and then would tell us how we were doing as compared to the average. He always seemed to be quite cheerful, but the bank manager was not. When there were several thousand pounds' worth of cheques floating around about to go into or come out of our bank account, some of them being depreciated at an apparently arbitrary rate fixed by our accountant for tax reasons, I became a bit lost. About the only way that I could tell if we were having a good year or a bad year was by what was being reported on the industry generally in the agricultural press.

My normal methods of good housekeeping went by the board. When the overdraft was standing at x thousand pounds, there seemed to be very little point in cutting down on cigarettes, when any saving would be cancelled out by one little pig turning up its toes. It seemed more sensible to chain smoke while battling to keep the little brute alive.

I found the accountancy side of pig farming baffling because of the amount of things that I could set against tax. There must be a reason why everyone in the country does not keep a sheep or a pig in the back garden and become self-employed, but God knows what it is. There were very few things that were definitely not allowable against tax. My attempts to include the TV licence because I watched the farming programmes on a Sunday gave the accountant a touch of indigestion, but the versatile pig seemed to be able to take care of everything else. At the end of the year a set of figures would be produced that made me wonder why the hell we were wasting our time playing at farming, but then we would realise that we had lived very comfortably during that year and appeared to have spent no money doing so.

Far and away the biggest debit item on our accounts was the meal bill. The salesman who has the job of shifting the stuff must have one of the most thankless tasks under the sun. He is under constant pressure from his bosses to sell animal feedstuffs and, at the same time, receives enormous stick from his customers because every visit seems to herald a rise in prices. I kept an eye on the price of pig feed over eight years during which time it went up just short of 450 per cent.

In Wales we were luckier than most because we were part of a mini co-operative when it came to buying feed. The fattener, Dick, and all his supplying farmers had clubbed together to buy feed as one unit and this protected us from the sharpest edge of inflation by enabling us to negotiate substantial discounts with the millers. I have always found it strange that farmers all over the country do not club together and force keener prices out of the suppliers. The British tradition of rugged individualism must add a comfortable 10 per cent to the farmers' costs.

The rep who sold us our feed became a friend, which is the sign of a good salesman. The poor man always seemed to come for his weekly visits when there was a large truck-load of straw to be unloaded or something, and he would be forced to roll up his sleeves and muck in. Buying animal feed is very like buying petrol. It is all very much the same although the firms involved in producing the stuff spend millions of pounds trying to persuade the farmer otherwise. The only incentive to buy our brand, excluding price, came at Christmas when the rep turned up with a tin of ginger biscuits. It was always much appreciated as we knew that the cost of it came out of his pocket rather than the company's.

The poor man used to attend his quarterly sales meetings with his bosses and come to us with his eyes sparking fire for a few weeks until he slipped back to normality. During the periods when he would zip round the kitchen like a firecracker he would try to sell us a bulk meal hopper. Compounders love selling these to pig and poultry farmers on hire purchase as it ties the farmer to the company's apron strings for however many years it takes to pay off the loan. The slopes and cracks of our yard were not really designed for the smooth running of trolleys laden with meal and so we never succumbed to these blandishments, preferring to hump bags around.

When we first moved in we had a visit from an irate meal company rep demanding to know why we had stopped buying feed from his firm and why we had stopped paying for our hopper. It emerged that our predecessor on the farm had bought one on HP a few months before he sold up and moved to New Zealand. He sold their hopper in his farm sale.

We always sought ways to augment our rather dicey income from pigs. One scheme which looked quite promising was building boarding kennels for dogs behind one of the barns. We had actually thought of converting one of the surplus barns into holiday accommodation but it was very difficult to put a price on a place whose main attraction was either the strong smell of pigs or a view over the slag heaps.

The kennel idea was sparked off by the vet. He had been about to start up some of his own having perceived a need in the area but he had met a girl who could think of better ways for him to spend his money and married him to show what she meant. Our application for planning permission did not get very far. Our nearest neighbours in the bungalows down below the lane were asked by the council if they had any objections. They had. One thought the dogs would have a detrimental effect on his wife's asthma; another thought they might escape and dig up his roses. We knew our pigs used to escape and do that sort of thing but surely not dogs. The grounds for one or two of the objections were so bizarre that we went to visit to find out what the fuss was all about.

Apparently one of them had tried to sell his house and had casually mentioned that we, who were a quarter of a mile away, kept pigs. The prospective buyer ran to his car making gagging noises. Once every three months when we moved the midden there was a bit of a pong but otherwise they can hardly have known we were there. Apart from the odd escaping pig. And the early morning feeding squeal. And perhaps the smell that some-times came from the stream which ran at the bottom of their gardens after we had used it.

The application was turned down but not before assorted plan-ners and health officials had had a good nose round the farm. The actual grounds for refusal were rather curious. By boarding dogs we would have destroyed the peace and tranquillity of the crematorium. I would have been perfectly happy to have taken a chance on the odd letter of complaint, no matter from where it was postmarked.

We got our revenge on the bungalows and kept them close to heel after that. We threatened to spread muck on the fields just behind the house if they ever stepped out of line again. One or two of them refused to be intimidated by even this threat. However, some research revealed that when the land on which their houses stood had been sold by my predecessor, the inhabitant of the farmhouse had reserved the right to order the removal of any garages, sheds and greenhouses backing onto the land if they were found to be offensive. That frightened off those who were still restive.

One piece of information revealed by the same research was suppressed. Our farm had never actually been sold away from the Big House. It had only been leased for 150 years at a peppercorn rent. We knew nothing about this and certainly had not been paying our peppercorn but, by the year 1990 when the lease runs out, it will be someone else's problem.

The land that used to belong to the farm was retained by the man who sold us the house and the buildings. He let it to a nearby dairy farmer who cut silage off it and ran bullocks and heifers up and down the side of the tips and occasionally came over to borrow ropes and things when they fell down abandoned mine shafts. We suited each other very well. He used our surplus buildings as catch pens if any of the bullocks proved unwilling to keep their date with the market or the slaughterhouse, and he cut our hedges in return.

He kept no pigs of his own which meant that our fences were lined with curious phalanxes of cattle watching the goings-on of the pigs with expressions of mild curiosity. On the frequent occasions when the pigs broke out there would be a rag-tag column of cattle dogging their footsteps. When I fooled the pigs into returning by yelling 'food,' the cattle would try to follow and would charge back through the pig-size holes in the hedges and gambol like gargantuan lambs all over the roses.

One aspect of living and working that close to the countryside for which we were not really prepared was the proximity of some of the wildlife. Birds nesting in the roof would have me scrabbling for the gun in the early hours of the morning, convinced that we were being invaded by the omnipresent burglars. A more curious happening took place when my wife took a couple of biscuits to bed with her to help ward off night starvation. In the morning they had disappeared without trace. We ringed the bed with rat traps and made sure that our toes did not poke out from underneath the blankets.

We had a sparrow that decided to excavate a hole underneath the gutter in order to build its nest. This may not sound a particularly noteworthy event, but the gutter was directly above the glass roof of our back porch. After the bird had broken two panes of glass by dropping boulders on them it was obviously time to clear it off the premises; but how? Throwing stones at it would do more damage than the bird itself. Saying 'Shoo' appeared to have no measurable effect. There was no way that I could stretch a ladder across the porch to lean against the wall. I had not even got a sparrowhawk to hand. In the end, we laid a sheet of hardboard across the roof until the sparrow had prepared its home to its own satisfaction.

For a couple of weeks a pair of bats took up residence in the top floor of the house and refused to be evicted. The first time we encountered them they were circling over the cot of our sleeping daughter, looking for the jugular vein. In the light of the moon they looked exceedingly sinister, and if one of them had suddenly turned into Christopher Lee we would not have been particularly surprised. We became quite fond of them in the end as they reduced the fly and mosquito population of the house to a minimum and also completely destroyed the dignity of the cats who were driven frantic by their habit of diving low in front of their noses and evading with effortless ease their fumbling attempts to catch them.

We never seemed to have less than half a dozen cats freeloading on the farm. Cats, shit and overdrafts are the three things you can be sure of finding on every farm. One cat we brought up with us from Kent. Being an unreformed alley cat it was in its element and disappeared into the maze of rubbish dumps in the locality on the first of May each year and only returned to winter with us. The local policeman brought us one kitten in his helmet and it did not seem polite to refuse him. Another was found sitting in the bath one morning. How it came to be there we had no idea, but it stayed. Cats seemed to come but never to go.

The cats were also driven to distraction by a couple of young collared doves that we reared after their parents had come to a sticky end. These birds became absurdly tame. The cats would be sleeping off some orgy of wren-killing when the doves would discover them in their shady bower and clatter down for a bit of company, cooing adoringly. The cats would be completely nonplussed and would stalk off with the doves plodding determinedly after them. These birds became a bit of a problem because they would follow me round while I was mucking out, perch on the shovel and generally get under my feet and up my nose. It is difficult to lose one's temper and hit something that lovingly coos at you. They started to lay an incestuous second generation but the female made the mistake of falling in love with Fred, boar, and he ate her for his breakfast.

If I managed to keep my temper with the doves, I was never quite so good at controlling it with the pigs. Bernie eventually moved out and Ted and his wife moved into our annex for a period and looked after our pigs in lieu of rent. Whenever I found myself hopping round the yard clutching a bruised toe because I had lost my temper and booted a sow, I would know it was time for a break. I have enormous admiration for those farmers who slog on seven days a week for years, but I could have never been one of them. Without Ted to allow me a day or two off, the animals could have driven me insane.

The ways that a pig could annoy me were legion. She could refuse to dung anywhere but in her water trough. She could be the one sow that moved the line of feeders every morning by shoving her nose underneath and heaving. She could take a sneaky nip at her neighbour each day and eventually create an ulcer. There was one tricky sow who finally managed to sprint round the feeders when my back was turned and jump into the meal barrow. The meal barrow was an old pram which I had gutted; a couple of hundredweight of meal was well over the prescribed weight limit. She only managed to get her leap in once causing the total disintegration of the pram and a series of fluent curses from myself that brought angry complaints by telephone from the bungalows.

The sow tried to do this several more times and I shattered two very expensive meal scoops on her snout before she decided that the pain outweighed the pleasure and gave up. I learned that putting in the boot hurt the booter much more than the bootee. To prevent excessive pain - to me, not the sow - I adopted the fist rather than the foot as the instrument of discipline. This worked quite well until I found a sow busy chewing off her neighbour's ear in the feeders. I brought my clenched fist smartly down on the top of her head and, to my horror, she gave a gentle sigh and collapsed. I dragged her out of the feeders and into the nearby farrowing house and rushed in to call the vet. When I came back, she had found a nest of mice in a corner of the shed and was eating them. I booted her that time.

The mice were a real nuisance, especially in the mealhouse. If we shut one of the cats in with them it might catch one or two but would then lose interest and allow the mice to hang all manner of bells round its neck. Since the numbers of mice could be measured in scores, this was very little use. Poison never achieved very much. For a start, the mice lived deep inside the pile of meal bags and rarely emerged to look at any poison. Why should they, with all that tasty meal around providing an expensively calculated diet for both young mice and breeding pairs? Before the mice became wise to it we would organise a mammoth hunt when we came down to the last few bags. Execution would be fast and furious but they soon cottoned on and would retreat when we were down to the dregs of the meal, only returning when a new load was delivered.

Rats were much more exciting than mice and worthy of pitting one's wits against - the difference between petty thieves and master criminals. We never had any shortage of them bacause the surrounding mixture of rural slum, industrial monuments and rubbish tips provided an ideal habitat. The only time that a rat managed to penetrate the security screens that surrounded the mealhouse, it created mayhem by burrowing straight into a mound of paper sacks filled with meal and tossing out a couple of hundredweight of feed in order to make room for itself.

I locked the cats in overnight and found them cowering in a corner the next morning with rat footmarks all round them. It moved out only after I gave it the fright of its life. I caught it with its nose sticking out of a bag one morning when I was carrying a syringe with which I had been doctoring a sow. Having just seen the 'Magnificent Seven' for the eighth time the night before, I was James Coburn immediately and flicked the syringe at it. The needle stuck quivering into the wooden floor about half an inch in front of its nose. It was just as well that I missed. Had it been otherwise, nobody would ever have believed me.

Our only other rodent predators were field voles. We were never very good at keeping them under control. I would find one at the meal and smack it smartly on the head. Then I would find its nest with half a dozen young mewling and puking inside it. These would be carefully removed to the kitchen and reared to adulthood in a box filled with wood shavings. Then they would be released to go back into the mealhouse. Voles have the highly sophisticated defence mechanism of looking sweet.

Our luck with dogs was mixed. Every farm has to have dogs, mainly because a farm dog does not have to have a licence and if something is free, you must have it. The first, with whom Gruntle fell in love, was a great success. He came from the local animal shelter where we found him shivering in the back of his enclosure while his neighbour snarled and snapped and tried to get at him. His neighbour was a large bear with claws on it as long as my middle finger.

The dog was so relieved at being rescued from this psychotic Winnie the Pooh that it appeared to have mugged up the *Call of the Wild* and *Jock of the Bushveldt* to find out how he ought to behave. He spent the rest of his days going around looking noble and dignified, acting out the part of Man's Best Friend. His only lapse was in the prosecution of his hobby which was slinking down the drive and barking at the lovers who flocked like starlings on the verges by the edge of the stream on summer evenings. One couple parked their car in rather a soggy spot and were forced to abandon it, stuck fast in the mud, after the dog had disturbed them. The following morning the man, a local councillor, had to come to me to beg for a tow out from the dumper. He could not work out if I recognised him and was too terrified to ask in case I did.

We obtained the dog a wife - a springer spaniel which, like all its breed, would have been better off inside a mental institution. Her owner gave her to us for nothing which we thought a little odd as she described her as being 'so friendly.' This strange creature slunk around the yard for most of the day, eating muck. If you stroked her, she would roll over on her back and pee, rubbing it well in with frantic wrigglings of the tail.

She had only been on the farm for an hour when the air was split by the most horrendous series of screams. It was the dog and I was quite sure that Fred must have got hold of it and ripped off one of its legs. I ran to the source of the noise and there was Ted frantically stroking the brute. He was most contrite. His story was that he found her eating muck and told her sternly to desist whereupon she rolled over and started to scream. I gave him an accusing look and examined the dog for signs of boot-broken ribs.

Later that day, I found the dog digging in the dustbin and re-proved her. The beast rolled over and started to scream. I looked at her aghast while my wife ran from the house and gathered her into her bosom, shooting me a look that would have curled me up, had I a guilty conscience. The dog peed down the front of her shirt. She took her indoors and placed her on the floor whereupon she went over and stole some of the cats' food. My

140

wife said 'No' and over on her back the dog rolled, screaming. Ted, his wife, my wife and I gathered round and watched her. She howled away for two or three minutes and then got back to her feet and returned to the cats' food. We lived with this for a week before we found an old lady who was prepared to take her. The dog's one good point was that the yard was cleaner than it had ever been by the time she left.

The original dog was shot for chasing cattle. As the animal lived in amiable proximity with the cattle just across the fence it was unlikely that he would go and chase someone else's. However, the farmer was within his rights to shoot straying dogs on his property although our relationship was rather strained after that. His successor was equally badly bred, extremely stupid and suited us very well. Being a lonely soul, he would make friends with any other animal around and was deeply wounded when the pigs failed to respond to his overtures. He took to collecting young rabbits from the surrounding countryside which he would bring into the house and lick adoringly on the carpet. The rabbits would eventually recover from the terror of capture and hop out the back door with the dog gazing mournfully after them.

One of the most wasteful aspects of pig farming seemed to me to be the disposal of the dead. A large pig was not too bad as there was always the knacker who was willing to turn its remains into cat food or glue. The really small pig, particularly those born dead, just used to end up on the midden. We considered various other solutions, such as storing them in the deepfreeze until we had accumulated sufficient numbers to present them to the biology departments of local schools to give the pupils a change from dissecting the eternal frog. Unfortunately none of the teachers seemed to be prepared to take the responsibility of making a decision. However we managed to solve the problem by buying a boa constrictor.

A boa should be an important part of running a pig farm. Ours was a remarkably efficient and cost-effective animal. It was a birthday present to me from my wife and arrived in a mini with a couple of friends so that the seller could give us a choice. We were told that it was a male and that snakes did not suffer from repressed libidos. We took the vendor's word for it as the beast had no visible signs of sex. We bought him at six feet long and he consumed a dead piglet every fortnight in one gigantic gulp. The economics were interesting. When we bought him, boas were selling at five pounds a foot. When we sold him, he had grown to about ten feet, fuelled entirely by dead piglets and we sold him for £115. If only pigs had been as profitable.

He spent most of his day living in an old fish tank on the windowsill. When he first arrived he tended to escape and we would find him draped round a roof beam or half-way up a chimney. He soon got over this phase and did nothing at all except eat his piglet every other Saturday and drop his most astonishingly large and smelly turd from no visible orifice the following Wednesday. Sometimes we would let him out for a bit of a slither because we could not help thinking that his life must have been crashingly dull. He used to like the occasional swim in the bath and he would drape himself over the back of the sofa while we watched television. He would follow the dog round with a hungry look in his eye but, apart from once biting a rather pig-like guest, he gave us no trouble at all.

We came to accept his presence as being perfectly normal and forgot about the effect that he could have on anyone who was unaware that he was around. One of his favourite resting places was curled round the wooden chandelier in the sitting room, where he would sit for days at a time, following the goings-on below him with a beady, unwinking eye. Once he was up there we frequently forgot about him.

One rather pompous couple came to stay with us for the weekend from London. Conversation after dinner on these occasions often had a certain predictability.

'Don't you feel that you are turning into a bit of a vegetable out in the sticks like this?'

My wife and I exchanged a weary glance. 'No, not really,' I

replied.

'But I feel that I must spend my life doing something worth-while.'

'Like stockbroking?'

'Yes, like stockbroking. I'm doing an important job financing industry.'

'Good.'

'But you, messing about with pigs. You could have been in charge of an account at the agency, by now. It's such a waste.'

'Don't worry, I'm quite happy,' I said, getting up to put another log on the fire.

'But we're right at the centre of things in London. It's really exciting.'

His wife joined in. 'But it's so nice to get into the country sometimes. Poor Peter has a two-hour commute every morning. You must admit, dear, that life in the country does have its compensations.'

'Oh, of course,' Peter agreed patronisingly. 'Do you know, I've now got an office on the third floor? Well, share an office actually. But it's quite big.'

'Yes,' said his wife. 'Peter's doing awfully well. He might be a partner in ten years.'

'Gosh,' said I, pouring out the whisky. The subject inevitably moved on to the excruciating questions of Life, the Universe and Everything.

'My own Truth juxtaposes Nietzsche and Empedocles.'

'Good.'

'I mean,' Peter continued as my eyes glazed over, 'we are only on this planet for a short time and it is vital to believe in one's own concepts of reality. Don't you agree?'

'Oh, quite,' I said, wondering if Bert the boar would be up to a quick bit of nookie in the morning.

'The seminal forces which dominate us depend on the id's relationship with the Universe. You have form because I believe you have form.'

143

'How interesting. Would you like a coffee?'

'Oh, thank you.' Peter was a bit put out because just as he was grasping for the ultimate concept I and my wife escaped to the kitchen while his own wife went to the loo.

'What an ass,' said my wife. 'I had forgotten that he was that bad.'

'Yes. I've noticed that when Londoners start to think great thoughts their utterances always achieve the clarity of a Newfoundland fog.'

'Perhaps he was right after all,' said my wife gloomily. Living among pigs does turn your brain to porridge.' I was just considering that worrying idea when there were yells of panic from the sitting room. We rushed back and there was Peter standing on the sofa, hurling cushions at one of the armchairs. His wife was right behind us.

'What on earth do you think you're doing, Peter?' she asked.

Peter was babbling in horror. 'There's a bloody monster behind that chair. It jumped at me from the ceiling.'

'What?'

'You heard me. A dirty great serpent. At least thirty feet long.'

'Are you all right, dear?' asked his wife anxiously.

'Of course I'm bloody all right. Get out of here before it attacks you.'

This was lovely. We had forgotten about the boa. When it became tired of the chandelier it would drop with a thump to the carpet, go underneath the chair, slip through a hole in the hessian base and curl up amid the springs in its interior. It was always a bit of a sod to get it out again. I strolled over to the chair.

'Behind this chair?'

'Yes, for Christ's sake be careful. It's right behind it.' Peter was still ensconced on his sofa with his last cushion held protectively over his balls. I moved the chair. There was nothing there.

'I think it's time for bed, dear.'

'It was there, I'm telling you. Huge it was, and it sort of slunk

144

along the floor.'

I tipped the chair up carefully so I would not disturb the snake and showed the bare floor beneath.

'Well, I'm afraid your monster seems to have vanished.'

'But it must have had form because Peter believed it had form,' put in my wife, helpfully.

'Oh shut up,' said Peter. 'I'm telling you there was a bloody great snake there.'

Peter was led snivelling from the room. Wickedly, we did not put him out of his misery until the morning he left. It saved us a fortune on whisky for the rest of the weekend and it was his last visit.

Money for Old Rope?

At the beginning of 1974 our accountant called us into a meeting. He read us the facts of life. We were paying rather more than we should have done for the privilege of keeping pigs. The overdraft which had been coasting downwards had suddenly started to climb. The accountant's advice was to sell up and start again somewhere else.

We held a conference that evening during Coronation Street and examined his reasoning. Our house had tripled in value since we had bought it less than three years earlier. Its value lay in that it was a reasonably pleasant country house, if you ignored the slag heaps, rather than a pig farm. We were scratching a living in a set of buildings that had a market value of virtually nothing while the house was worth a substantial sum of money. It seemed that the financial balance of the enterprise was the wrong way round. It would be better to sell up and try to find a reasonable house where it would be possible to put a large amount of capital into good new stock and a purpose-built set of pig buildings.

We were aware that money spent on our existing set-up would be money that we would never get back. Any increase in the quantity or further specialisation into pig accommodation would, if anything, detract from the value of the property as a whole. The next man in would probably bulldoze the lot and build himself a swimming pool.

The next move in our expansion would have required substantial amounts of capital sunk outside in the yard - capital that we did not have and were not too enthusiastic about borrowing at crippling rates of interest. I was spending too much time dabbling around in slurry and not enough in thinking and planning. To install proper slurry tanks, although gladdening the heart of the health inspector, would have cost too much.

The main problem was that modern pig farming had become a finely balanced science. Profit and loss depended on fractional differences in the animals' ability to convert cereal-based feeds into meat. Our buildings were constructed for cows. They were large, draughty and poorly insulated. They would do at a pinch when the industry was doing well, but when margins were tight any profits were swallowed up by the pigs using feed to keep warm rather than converting it into meat.

So we decided to sell the farm and start again. Next time we would have a better idea of what we wanted to do and, starting with a clean site and a new herd, we would have little difficulty in making ourselves the fortune that had so far eluded us.

We found that the path to big money was no smoother than the path to true love. For the sake of our fattener, we decided to run down the herd over several months in order to give him the time to find an alternative source of supply. We found a local farmer who dealt in pigs and he was able to dispose of some of our more clapped-out matrons and find new breeding niches for the younger sows that were still in full production. Duke went to enjoy a contented retirement with a field to himself and a private harem of five nubile young sows whom he could flatten to his heart's content. Alf went to improve the quality of Cornish weaners.

The sow buyer came one Saturday morning to negotiate a price on our four remaining adult animals. He had taken the other sows as we weaned the litters from them and we were virtually cleaned out apart from young stock. A price was agreed and he was to come on Monday to remove them. Dick was also due to take away eighty rather overweight stores. At 9 am on Sunday we received a visit from the Ministry of Agriculture instead. The buyer's herd had gone down with swine vesicular disease and, since we had had recent contact with him, we were placed under a restriction order forbidding the movement of stock from the premises.

A restriction order was one of the problems that beset the farmer for which Ted had prepared me fairly thoroughly. He had grim memories of the big foot and mouth outbreak during the sixties. Ted had been the only farmer for miles around whose stock had not caught the disease and movement of animals from his farm had been forbidden for something like six months. Pigs did not stop growing or being born just because a bit of paper said that they could not be shifted and, by the time that Ted was halfway through the six months, he was down on his knees praying for foot and mouth.

He had pigs in the lavatories, in the garage and in the greenhouse and was thinking about vacating the ground floor of his house to give them more room. That outbreak may have cost the government scores of millions of pounds in compensation to those farmers whose stock caught the disease, but Ted's gargantuan overweight and over-age pigs gave the millers some consolation.

Ted's advice was to hurry up and catch SVD before the pigs ate me out of existence. The authorities were full of advice on how to avoid the disease but not very forthcoming on how to catch it. Anyway, we only had a couple of hundred piglets and plenty of room for growth owing to the absence of sows. We would have to raise the eighty largest stores to pork weight at least which was an expensive nuisance, and we had four sows that had already been sold. Spending money on feeding them would bring nothing at all back. Our meal rep thought that this was poetic justice. By selling up, we were depriving him of a substantial order so it was only fair that we would have to increase our purchase over the last month and get very little back ourselves.

Apart from him, the only people who got any satisfaction out of the restriction order were the Ministry vets who drank endless cups of tea both before and after examining the animals for signs of the dreaded pox. The stores did not like their calls at all. They stood in their pens and watched with growing apprehension as the vets donned vast quantities of waterproof clothing and then vigorously brushed each other down with buckets full of foul-smelling disinfectant. Then, dripping, they would enter the pen crackling and rustling like frigates in full sail. The pigs would scream their dismay, convinced that the slaughterer was on them before their time and leap over walls, troughs and each other in their efforts to escape.

The four sows never let the vets close enough to examine them. I put them in a paddock where they could eat grass and resolved to let them get on with the business of staying alive by themselves. I felt rather guilty about them and took to slipping them buckets of meal on the side. My wife did the same without telling me and the buyer turned out to have detailed a friend to do the same over the roadside fence every afternoon. They could only waddle when they were taken away.

At the end of the month we were declared free of possible infection despite Ted's dire warnings and we set about selling the porkers. Dick wanted some of them but the largest fifty-five were too big for him. He arranged for a dealer to come over and have a look at them. The dealer arrived in a large red Mercedes and went over to the pen to examine the pigs. He dusted the top of the wall and leant his elbows on it, being careful not to mark the suede of his coat.

'How many do you say there are here?'

'Fifty-five.'

'Humph. They're so small that there don't look to be as many as that.'

'Do you want me to run them through the scales?'

'No. It's not worth it. How much do you want for them?'

'Nine-fifty?' Nine hundred and fifty pounds was a little optimistic but it gave me a reasonable profit. It worked out at £17.25 per pig.

He nearly choked. 'Nine-fifty? You're joking. Do you think I'm made of bloody money. Nine-fifty. Cor love me. If I paid that sort of money for a bunch of knock-kneed screws like these, my family would be out in the bloody street. I bought a bunch of pigs near Newcastle last week. Sweet round little buggers they were, not like these and I paid seven-fifry. And there were sixty of them.'

'Well I'm certainly not letting you have these for that sort of money.'

'No, I can see you won't, you miserable git. Are you prepared to come down to a reasonable price?'

He was beginning to depress me. 'Make me an offer,' I said.

'Eight?'

'No.'

'Oh come on. I've driven fifty bloody miles to do you a favour. You've got to give me some sort of profit. It's cost me a fortune to get here and I expect you're the sort of bloke who'll expect me to pay for the lorry that takes them away.'

'That's right.'

'Look. Just so's I don't waste any more of my precious time, I'll tell you what I'll do. I'll give you nine for them.'

'Done.' We shook hands on it. It was only a pound less per pig than I was asking so I was quite pleased.

'Right, the lorry will be round for them in the morning. I suppose you'll want to be paid now?'

'That's right.'

He sighed. 'God, you're a hard man.' He opened his cheque-book and leaned on the bonnet of his car. 'Right then, that's fifty five pigs at nine pounds per pig, that's....er....£495.'

'Hang on a minute. I think there's a bit of a misunderstanding.'

'Misunderstanding? What do you mean. You're bloody robbing me. Robbing me.'

'By nine, I thought that you meant nine hunderd pounds the lot. I was asking for nine hundred and fifty pounds.'

'Oh. Not nine pounds fifty pence each?'

'No.'

'Would you take eight hundred and fifty quid?'

'Yes.' He filled out the cheque and scuttled down the drive. I felt as big a twit as he must have done.

With the pigs out of the way we started to sell most of the equipment in preparation for the house sale. It went mostly to neighbours but some we held on to for our next venture. We found that we owned thirty-six galvanised iron pig troughs in rather dubious condition. How we came to have that many I could not imagine as they are pretty useless things at the best of times. They had been shut up in a shed for some time so it may have been by a process of natural reproduction.

On the advice of the estate agent we spent a few satisfying hours destroying all the easily removable evidence of pig occupation such as chewed insulation and middens so that potential buyers would not feel that they had to set up a pig breeding unit. That done, we sat back to wait for the flood of those with bulging wallets and a love of unusual vistas to come running round.

They came, too, in large quantities. Being the owners of a curious property - a large house, dozens of buildings and virtually no land - we had some rather odd people turning up. One man came from the USA, from Chicago, to be precise - as was so obvious from his wide-brimmed felt hat and broad-lapelled, loud, striped suit. This Capone wanted to turn the place into one of those hideous medieval banqueting set-ups, although it required a real visionary to be able to translate the weaner pool into a crenellated castle frowning over the satanic landscape.

Another wanted to turn all the barns into bijou executive residences and transform the place into a Volvo-ridden colony of those who should have known better. The buyer himself was going to act as gardener and security guard. The offer that we eventually accepted was from a man who wanted to stuff his decaying mother-in-law into the annex and use her money to set up a duplicating and printing business in the farrowing house. The planning office agreed that this was a reasonable scheme and so we sat back to count our chickens and work out the most inflation-proof method of investing our millions. The contracts were to be exchanged on a Saturday.

Unfortunately the local paper came out on a Friday. In that Friday's edition, there was an exciting lead story. The bypass that entombed the remains of our burnt barn was to be extended. The civil servants were going to allow public participation in choosing the route that the road should take and had published two alternatives. One route would cost nine million pounds and continue straight on from where the road currently left off through the slag heaps and rubbish tips and bother nobody. The other route cost ten million and would start off with a tight hairpin bend so that it could sweep across the crematorium, bungalows and our yard and then on through a couple of villages, demolishing sixty-odd houses as it went. Our buyer withdrew his offer and hurriedly disappeared back into the hinterland, squeaking with relief at his narrow escape from being motorwayed.

So what were we to do? The first thing was to attend the public exhibition which was being held locally so that the planners could graphically show the terrible destruction that would result if the route across our farm was chosen. Along with 98 per cent of the native population we voted for the other route, the only dissent coming from those who made their living totting and rat-catching amid the rubbish tips. Then we checked with the civil servant in charge who told us that the route across our farm would not be chosen but it would be a year or so before the government would make the announcement to that effect.

How were we supposed to find a buyer for the place with the threat of a road hanging over it? I contacted our lawyer and he beavered happily and expensively away in murky realms of planning blight and summoned us in to tell us the result of his labours. In a year's time when a definite route was announced, we could force the government to buy the farm if its saleability was impaired. Until then, to quote his own legal turn of phrase, we were in the shit. Not for the first time in my life I pondered the delights of going up to London for the day to throw stones through the windows of offices in Whitehall.

We kept the farm on the market but we were now looking for a buyer who not only had money but was either an idiot or a gambler as well. Such people were uncommon and so we had to set about making a living once more until such a paragon should appear. The obvious solution, warmly advocated by the meal rep, was to buy in another load of pigs but most of our breeding equipment had been sold and, if we bought in animals to fatten, we would have been faced with the old problem of pouring feed into them merely in order to keep them warm.

For agricultural purposes, retired pig buildings appeared to have few uses. Most of the ways that they could have been put to work were ruled out because of the depressed state of agriculture, although there was nothing unusual about that. Since I have been in the business, the one time that the industry was not depressed was at half-past three in the afternoon of 2nd April 1977. Calves, at the time we were trying to fill our buildings, were being sold for pennies in the local market due to lack of confidence in the future of beef and the one obvious candidate to rent them, the farmer who ran his beefs in the neighbouring fields, was in a bigger financial pickle than ourselves.

We tried advertising stable accommodation for horses. We had one applicant with no money. She had gone to the pony sales with her father and, when his back was turned, she had stuck up her hand and become the owner of a small foul-tempered stallion with nowhere to house it. The best place for the beast would have been inside some tins of dog food but we took pity on its owner and let it roam the building in solitary spendour in exchange for a bit of baby-sitting from its owner.

It was a perfectly horrid little brute which confirmed my life-time aversion to horses as stupid, useless and highly dangerous animals with permanent expressions of quite unjustifiable arrogance. It developed a remarkable accuracy for kicking me in the most vulnerable spot any time that I happened to stray within range. It also became an escapologist, carrying on the tradition that the pigs had established. The difference was that, where the pigs went under or straight through any obstructions, the stallion went over the top which required a complete readjustment in outlook from the jailer. Where previously I had walked round the farm with my nose to the ground looking for holes, I now had to break the habit of years and look up instead.

Ted and his wife had moved out by this time and bought themselves a house about twenty-five miles away so that we could offer the premises without a sitting tenant. This had left us with an empty annex and that surely could be turned into holiday accommodation and therefore more money. I checked with the lawyer about kicking holiday tenants out if they looked like sticking and also about the dangers of misrepresentation in advertising. If we advertised it truthfully as having a fine view over the slag heaps we would not have been overwhelmed by the rush of applicants. He gave us the all clear and we filled the annex with furniture harvested from some of the more salubrious rubbish dumps and topped up with oddments from the local salerooms. We then advertised in the very best papers and waited.

We were only sorry that we had not started holiday letting when we first moved in. It was money for old rope. The only breakage was one tea cup, and the breaker was so abject at having bust up the set that he bought an entire tea service to replace it. Since the one he broke came in exchange for half a dozen cereal packet tops it was rather embarrassing. From the point of view of our daughter, married couples with children were the best holidaymakers as they provided a source of playmates. From the point of view of the garden, elderly couples just short of complete decrepitude were best. One ancient pair started off in the vegetable garden and spent their entire week digging through to the roses. Since that part of the garden had been neglected for two years, it was very helpful. The next couple planted rows of cauliflowers and other goodies because they could not bear to see the good earth standing idle.

Another couple had an adult son who was seized by an urge to paint a picture of our outbuildings. He and his parents borrowed brushes from me and virtually whitewashed the lot until the artist was satisfied that they looked right. He was interested in the contrast between the white of the buildings and the overwhelming black of the mountains of coal that were the backdrop.

The only real problem that turned up from the holiday lets

was the loo. It had long been a source of irritation to us that our half of the house had a bathroom that must have been installed during the reign of Queen Victoria while, in the annex, everything was a modern gleaming yellow and the walls were covered in tiles, cupboards and all the things that went to make a really mod con.

The second day of our first week of letting, the guest timidly knocked on the door and announced that his loo was blocked. It was one of those modern, rather splashy, shallow-pan jobs that are supposed to drain away rather than flush with a Niagara-like roar as did our own. Upon investigation, it was observed that it was not completely blocked but seeped in a rather sinister fashion. There was clearly a fundamental obstruction. The first thing to do was to poke around a bit. I despatched the guest to root out various lengths of wire, unravelled coat hangers, curtain wires and the like, and I used his finds to rummage around in the nether regions of the loo without much success. The trouble stemmed from the bend which was not so much a 'u' but a 'z.'

The guest by this time was feeling decidedly guilty and his wife had fled the house for fear of what we might find to be the root of the obstruction. He suggested that a hose might be worth trying and so we carefully fed one down the pan and turned it on. That did not work either and we called a ten-minute recess while the guest mopped up the resultant mess. It was then decided to call in the plumber.

Plumber One could come in a week. Plumber Two in a fortnight. I explained that there was some degree of urgency and Plumber Two suggested that I call my old friend the Health Inspector. The first time I called him, he was at lunch. The second time I was left hanging on for twenty minutes while someone went to check the worksheets. I hung up. The third time I called there was no reply. The next plumber I called could come within two hours. Marvellous. The snag was that there was a minimum charge for the visit. There are certain circumstances where one is not really in a position to argue - particularly as the guest was beginning to hop from one foot to the other.

The plumber came armed with a well-used plunger and a strong smell. Within fifteen seconds he had the thing working and was strolling back to his van with a merry whistle and a bundle of notes from me. All was well for two days until the tenant knocked on the door again. The loo had given a throaty cough and choked itself once more. The guest had already bought his own plunger but, however hard we plunged it, nothing seemed to happen. Washing soda and boiling water would not shift it, in spite of the maker's promises, nor would prayer.

The ultimate loo unblocker turned out to be silage additive. Scattered round most farmyards are a variety of plastic drums marked 'poison' or 'corrosive.' I went and tapped a variety of these evil-smelling chemicals from dumps on a friend's farm and liberally dosed the loo with each of them in turn. It lapped them all up until I used the silage additive. There was a pained hiss and the loo never dared to block itself again.

It would be dangerous to give a blanket recommendation to this method as, in the long run, the loo might well crumble and the sewers collapse but, provided everything is well insured, it is well worth a try. That lavatorial trauma apart, the guests were pure profit and I was able to spend the rest of my time trying to earn a crust. I started off in a factory and was rapidly fired as the damage I managed to create soon far outweighed any profit that the company could have made from my services. Next I was able to return to my native element in the form of an enormous pile of dung on the farm of a neighbour and whiled away the weeks sculpting it into artistic shapes and hurling it through shed windows. It was when I was away enjoying myself at this that my wife managed to sell the farm to a couple of teachers for only 40 per cent less than our pre-motorway asking price.

What did we get out of three years of pigs? First and foremost we managed to make a living of sorts and fill our lungs with the fine fresh air of the country, redolent with the smells of pigshit and, on windy days, black with coal dust. We gained our independence. The delights of not having a human boss to please have to be experienced to be appreciated. Within limitations, we could do what we liked when we liked. We had a regular trickle of people coming to stay from London. They would arrive, whey-faced, and talked about their prospects for promotion, commuting problems and mortgages, all of which gave me a reminiscent shudder and the opportunity to marvel at the resilience of the human race that they are prepared to live out their one life under those sorts of pressures.

To be a successful pig farmer, rather than a mere pig farmer, you need an almost endless list of qualities, very few of which we possessed. The most important requirement is inexhaustible patience. You cannot, or rather you should not, scream at or hit a pig just because it is naughty. Pigs die, refuse to eat, eat too much, break out of their pens, sit on their young, get diarrhoea or do any one of the thousand and one things that they dream up for the sole purpose of driving their owner to distraction. Without patience, your pigs will either end up dead, which does not help the profits, or be so terrified of you that they will be totally unmanageable and that does not help the profits either.

In addition to being patient, you need certain skills. You need to be a stockman, a vet, builder, mechanic, financier, welder, plumber, electrician, salesman and a line in arson would be no hindrance either. If you can do all these things, you should make a reasonable living. If you can't, life can be a lot more interesting.

Pig farming can be a social embarrassment as well. You usually carry olfactory or living evidence of your calling round with you. The most hideous of such occasions was the one time I donned a dinner jacket during my career as a pig farmer. It was to go to the annual National Farmers' Union dance and I was seated next to my solicitor's wife being as witty and charming as only a pig farmer can. During cheese a pig louse fell out of my hair and on to her side plate.

Pig lice are one of the occupational hazards and one soon became used to brushing them off if the louse powder had not been used recently. This one sat on the plate and grinned at my partner. A pig louse compared with a good old human nit, is King Kong to a chimp. This one looked like King Kong's elder brother. She saw it and screamed before I could squash it with my thumb. Her husband became abusive and my wife and I slunk out of a side door and away to avoid the resultant confusion and recriminations. He sent me a letter a few days later telling me to seek my legal advice elsewhere.

This is the sort of hazard that making your living from stock farming can all too easily create. Three years of pig farming taught us no sort of lesson. We had casually fallen into pigs as our first agricultural line. When we sold the farm, we did not do the sensible thing and reinvest in pigs. At least we knew something about the beasts by that stage. But that would have been too logical. We became dairy farmers instead.

ANY FOOL CAN BE A.....
DAIRY FARMER

By

JAMES ROBERTSON

James Robertson set out for the beautiful, badger-haunted fields of Devon to turn grass into gold via the medium of milk. It only took an encounter with his first cow to realise that he would need the survival instincts of the SAS if he were to live to appreciate this rural idyll.

His cows did not seem to live up to their public image of placid benevolence and created a working environment as ruthless as that of the London advertising agency from which he had escaped. There were cows with sharpshooter hooves, an amorous bull set on enjoying the favours of a neighbour's herd - or even those of the farmer himself, should he turn his back - and the terrible tyranny of a new-born calf.

ISBN 9781904871729

Published by The Good Life Press Ltd.

The Good Life Press Ltd.
The Old Pigsties
Clifton Fields
Lytham Road
Preston PR4 0XG
01772 633444

The Good Life Press Ltd. publishes a wide range of titles for the smallholder, 'goodlifer' and farmer. We also publish **Home Farmer,** the monthly magazine for anyone who wants to grab a slice of the good life - whether they live in the country or the city. Other titles of interest include: